THE GOSPEL OF GOD

Romans

A BIBLE STUDY ON ROMANS FOR WOMEN

VOLUME 1 OF 2 / ROMANS 1:1-8:39

KERI FOLMAR

To my parents, Gary and Adele Harrison:
May the God of hope fill you with all joy and peace
in believing, so that by the power of the Holy Spirit
you may abound in hope.

CRUCIFORM PRESS

CruciformPress.com | info@CruciformPress.com

Praise for Keri Folmar's *Delighting in the Word* Inductive Bible Studies for Women

"With simple clarity, Keri Folmar guides us in learning to study the Bible … Keri encourages us to read God's Word carefully, to understand clearly, and to apply prayerfully … she encourages her readers first and foremost to listen well to God's inspired word."
> **Kathleen Nielson** is author of the *Living Word Bible Studies*; Director of Women's Initiatives, The Gospel Coalition; and wife of Niel, who served as President of Covenant College, 2002 to 2012.

"Keri's Bible studies will not only bring the truths of Scripture to bear upon your life, but will also train you up for better, more effective study of any book of the Bible with her consistent use of the three questions needed in all good Bible study: Observation, Interpretation, and Application."
> **Connie Dever** is author of *The Praise Factory* children's ministry curriculum and wife of Mark, senior pastor of Capitol Hill Baptist Church and President of 9Marks.

"It is hard to imagine better inductive Bible study tools than these. So many study tools wander from the biblical text, but Keri Folmar's studies concentrate on what the biblical author says … unfolding its message with accuracy and clarity."
> **Diane Schreiner**, the wife of SBTS professor, author, and pastor Tom Schreiner and mother of four grown children, has led women's Bible studies for more than 20 years.

"No clever stories, ancillary anecdotes, or emotional manipulation here. Keri takes us deeper into the text, deeper into the heart of the biblical author, deeper into the mind of Christ, and deeper into our own hearts … these are great studies to do on your own or with others."
> **Kristie Anyabwile** is a North Carolina native and graduate of NC State University with a degree in history. Her husband, Thabiti, serves as a pastor in Washington, DC, and as a Council Member for The Gospel Coalition.

"Keri is convinced that God is God-centered and that for the sake of our joy, we should be, too … She skillfully created these rich resources — and not only that, she has put the tools in your hands so you can study God's word for yourself … I highly recommend that you embark on these studies with some other ladies. Then you can all watch in amazement at how God gives you contentment in him."
> **Gloria Furman** is a pastor's wife in the Middle East, and author of *Glimpses of Grace, Treasuring Christ When Your Hands Are Full*, and *The Pastor's Wife*.

CONTENTS

Bible Studies for Women

All new covers coming soon!

10 weeks

Joy! (Philippians)

10 weeks

Faith (James)

10 weeks

Grace (Ephesian

11 weeks

11 weeks

9 weeks

Son of God (Gospel of Mark, 2 volumes)

Zeal (Titus)

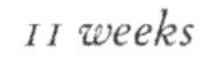

The Gospel of God - A Bible Study on Romans for Women (Vol. 1)

Print / PDF ISBN: 978-1-949253-39-9

INTRODUCTION: WHY STUDY THE BIBLE?

As we begin this study of Paul's letter to the church at Rome, we should think through why we are studying the Bible. Why not read some other book? Or why not just get together with some other women and chat?

Well, have you heard the story about the kindergarten teacher who had her class paint pictures of anything they chose? After observing a little girl who was working very intently on her painting, the teacher asked, "What are you painting?" The girl answered, "It's a picture of God." Amused, the teacher informed her, "No one knows what God looks like." Without looking up from her painting, the little girl responded, "They will in a minute!"

This might be a cute example of a precocious child, but many people paint pictures of God in their own minds. They "know" that God is a certain way, because they want him to be that way.

However, the one true God is transcendent. He is beyond our capacity to know. First Timothy 6:16 describes God, "[W]ho alone has immortality, who dwells in unapproachable light, whom no one has ever seen or can see." God existed before time. He is the Creator, and we are his creatures. Sinful man cannot approach the holy God.

How can we know this God if we cannot approach him? He has to approach us. The only way to truly know God is for him to reveal himself to us. He reveals his existence and power in creation. (See Psalm 19 and Romans 1:18–21.) However, if we want to truly know God in a personal way, it must be through his Word.

And God **wants** us, his creatures, to know him. Jeremiah 9:23–24 says:

> Thus says the LORD: "Let not the wise man boast in his wisdom, let not the mighty man boast in his might, let not the rich man boast in his riches, but let him who boasts boast in this, that he understands

and knows me, that I am the Lord who practices steadfast love, justice, and righteousness in the earth."

Do you boast in understanding and knowing the Lord? Do you want to know this God who practices love, justice, and righteousness in the earth? He wants you to understand and know him. He is ready to speak to you every morning when you wake up… throughout the day… and before you go to bed. You have only to open his Word.

A well-known catechism says, "The chief end of man is to glorify God and enjoy him forever." That is what we were created for—to truly know and enjoy the God of the universe. Jeremiah the prophet cried out: "Your words were found, and I ate them, and your words became to me a joy and the delight of my heart."

The great preacher, C.H. Spurgeon, said:

> Believer! There is enough in the Bible for you to live upon forever. If you should outnumber the years of Methuselah, there would be no need for a fresh revelation; if you should live until Christ should return to the earth, there would be no necessity for the addition of a single word; if you should go down as deep as Jonah, or even descend as David said he did, into the depths of hell, still there would be enough in the Bible to comfort you without a supplementary sentence. (https://spurgeon.org/sermons/0005.htm)

This is why we study the Bible: it is God's revelation of himself to us. We need to know who God truly is and guard against painting our own picture of him. God has revealed himself to us not in paintings but in the words of Scripture and ultimately in his Son. God, the Creator, has spoken, and we, his creation, should listen to his words as life-sustaining truth and joyfully obey them.

The purpose of this Bible study workbook is to assist you in studying Romans in an inductive way. Inductive Bible study is **reading the passage in context and asking questions of** the text with the purpose of deriving the meaning and significance from the text itself**. We do this automatically every day when we read the newspaper, blogs, or even recipes. When we study the Bible inductively we are after the author's original intent (what the author meant when he wrote the passage to his original audience). In this workbook, you will figure out the author's meaning by answering a series of questions about the text while paying close attention to the words and context of the passage. After figuring out the meaning of the text, there will be questions to help you apply it to your life.

As you read through Romans 1–8, may the Holy Spirit give you a deeper understanding of the gospel, which is "the power of God for salvation to everyone who believes" (Romans 1:16), and may that understanding result in joy that overflows to the glory of God.

How to Do Inductive Bible Study

Step 1 – Begin with prayer. "Open my eyes, that I may behold wondrous things out of your law" (Psalm 119:18).

Step 2 – Read the text.

Step 3 – Observation. *The goal of this step is to figure out what the text is saying.* These questions should be answered from the very words of the text.

Step 4 – Interpretation. *The goal of this step is to figure out what the text meant to the original hearers.* It is easy to skip this most important step. However, incorrect interpretation leads to incorrect application. We cannot understand what God is saying to us if we don't first understand *what* he was saying to the original audience, and *why* he was saying it.

Your job in interpretation is to figure out the main point of the passage and understand the arguments that support the main point. Your interpretation should flow out of your observations, so keep asking yourself, "Can I support this interpretation based on my observations?"

Step 5 – Application. *Prayerfully apply the passage to your own life.* The application should flow from the main point of the text.

Keep God's Redemptive Plan in Mind

Luke 24:44–47 says,

> Then [Jesus] said to them, "These are my words that I spoke to you while I was still with you, that everything written about me in the Law of Moses and the Prophets and the Psalms must be fulfilled." Then he opened their minds to understand the Scriptures, and said to them, "Thus it is written, that the Christ should suffer and on the third day rise from the dead, and that repentance for the forgiveness of sins should be proclaimed in his name to all nations, beginning from Jerusalem."

We study the Bible so that we can know Christ, repent, be forgiven, and proclaim him to the nations. We must keep Jesus in mind when we study Scripture. Adrienne Lawrence writes, "God has one overarching redemptive plan—to glorify himself by creating and redeeming a people for himself through Christ. Christ is at the center of God's plan. All of Scripture in some way speaks to that plan. Keep this in mind as you are doing your study of Scripture."

[Note: This "how to" has been adapted from Adrienne Lawrence's pamphlet on Inductive Bible Study.]

Notes on This Study Guide

The first week of this inductive study will be an overview of Romans. In the following weeks you will study smaller segments of the letter and answer observation, interpretation, and application questions. The questions were written based on language from the English Standard Version of the Bible. However, you are welcome to use any reliable translation to do the study.

To assist you in recognizing the different types of questions asked, the questions are marked by the three different icons seen below.

Observation

Look closely at the text to figure out what it is saying. Get answers directly from the text, using the words of Scripture to answer the observation questions.

Interpretation

Determine the author's intended meaning by figuring out what the text meant to its original hearers.

Application

Based on the author's intended meaning, *apply* the passage to your own heart and life today.

Because Scripture interprets Scripture, many of the questions cite passages in addition to the one you are studying in Romans. If the question says, "Read…" you will need to read the additional verses cited to answer the question. If the question says, "See…" the additional verses will help you answer the question but are not necessary. "See also…" signals you to read the additional verses if you would like to study the answer to the question further.

You only need your Bible to do this study of Romans, and, in fact, I highly recommend first answering the questions directly from your Bible before looking at any other materials. That said, it might be helpful for you to confirm your answers, especially if you are leading others in a group study. To check your answers or for further study, there are good commentaries by Thomas R. Schreiner, John Murray, R.C. Sproul and John R.W. Stott. I also found *Teaching Romans* by Christopher Ash helpful in my studies.

To increase your enjoyment of studying the Bible, read my book, *The Good Portion: The Doctrine of Scripture for Every Woman*. For more instruction on how to study the Bible, read *Bible Study: Following the Ways of the Word*, by Kathleen Buswell Nielson, and *Dig Deeper! Tools to Unearth the Bible's Treasure*, by Nigel Beynon and Andrew Sach. Bible study teachers and students who want a better understanding of New Testament theology can read Thomas R. Schreiner's, *Magnifying God in Christ: A Summary of New Testament Theology*.

Notes for Leaders

This Bible study guide can be used by individuals alone, but the best context for Bible study is in the local church. Studying the Bible together promotes unity and ignites spiritual growth within the church.

The study was designed for participants to complete five days of "homework," and then come together to discuss their answers in a small group. The goal of gathering in small groups is to promote discussion among women to sharpen one another by making sure all understand the meaning of the text and can apply it to their lives. As women discuss, their eyes may be opened to applications of the text they didn't see while doing the study on their own. Believers will encourage one another in their knowledge of the gospel, and unbelievers will hear the gospel clearly explained. As a result, women will learn from one another and come away from group Bible study with a deeper understanding of the text and a better knowledge of how to read the Bible on their own in their private times of study and prayer.

If you are leading a small group, you will have some extra homework to do. **First, know what Bible study is and is not.** Bible study is not primarily a place to meet felt needs, eat good food and chat, receive counseling, or have a free–for–all discussion. Some of these things do happen in a women's Bible study, but they should not take over the focus. Studying the Bible means digging into the Scriptures to get the true meaning of the text and applying it to lives that change as a result.

Second, make sure you know the main points of the text before leading discussion by carefully studying the passage and checking yourself using a good commentary, like one of those listed above. You may also find a Bible dictionary and concordance helpful. Second Timothy 3:16–17 says, "All Scripture is breathed out by God and profitable for teaching, for reproof, for correction, and for training in righteousness, that the man [or woman] of God may be complete, equipped for every good work." Scripture is powerful. That power comes through truth. Scripture is not like a magical incantation: We say the words and see the effect. We must know what the text of Scripture means before we can faithfully apply it and see its work of transformation in our lives. Your job as a discussion leader is not to directly teach, nor to simply facilitate discussion, but rather to lead women in finding the meaning of the text and help them see how it is "profitable" and can make them "complete, equipped for every good work" (2 Timothy 3:16–17).

Third, pray. Pray for the women in your group during the week while you prepare. Pray as you start your small group study, asking the Holy Spirit to illuminate the Scripture to your minds and apply it to your hearts. And encourage women to pray at the end of your small group based on what they studied. Ask the Holy Spirit to use his sword, the Word of God, in the lives of the women you are leading.

Fourth, draw women into discussion and keep your discussion organized. Choose what you determine are the most important questions from the study guide, focusing the bulk of your discussion on the interpretation and application questions. Ask a question, but don't answer it! Be comfortable with long pauses or rephrase questions you think the group didn't understand. Not answering the questions yourself may be a bit awkward at first, but it will promote discussion in the end because the women will know they have to do the answering. Feel free to affirm good answers or sum up after women have had time to discuss particular questions. This gives clarity to the discussion. However, don't feel the need to fill in every detail and nuance you gleaned from your personal study. Your goal is to get your group talking.

Fifth, keep your focus on the Bible. The Holy Spirit uses the Scriptures to change women's hearts. Don't be afraid of wrong answers. Gently use them to clarify and teach by directing attention back to the text of Scripture for the right answer. If someone in your group goes off on unhelpful tangents, direct her back to the question and address the tangent later, one on one, or with reading material. However, if the tangent is on a vital question that goes to the gospel, take time to talk about it. These are God–given opportunities.

Sixth, be sure to discuss the gospel. In your prep time, ask yourself what the text has to do with the gospel and look for opportunities to ask questions to bring out the gospel. Hopefully, your church members will invite unbelievers to your study who will hear the glorious good news. But, even if your group is made up of all believers, we never get beyond our need to be reminded of Christ crucified and what that means for our lives.

Lastly, enjoy studying the Scriptures with your group. Enjoy studying Romans! Your love and passion for the Word of God will be contagious, and you will have the great joy of watching your women catch it and rejoice in the Word with you.

Paul's Letter to the Church at Rome

The apostle Paul was a former Pharisee who had persecuted the church. His life was transformed when he was personally commissioned by the risen Jesus to take the gospel to the Gentiles—the non–Jewish peoples (see Acts 9). Paul then traveled the known world, spreading the gospel and planting churches. While Paul knew many of the believers in Rome (see chapter 16), he had not planted the church. He wrote the letter to the Roman church probably around A.D. 57 toward the end of his life.

Christians met together in Rome from very early on. Originally, the church was likely made up of Jewish converts. Over time, Gentiles in Rome also became Christians. In A.D. 49 the Roman emperor Claudius commanded all Jews to leave Rome (Acts 18:2). Over time, some of the Jewish Christians returned to Rome, so the church was made up of both Jews and Gentiles.

Paul's letter to the Roman church is his longest and most theologically comprehensive letter. However, it is not meant to be a systematic theology. It has a pastoral purpose as a missionary letter. Paul expounds the gospel in the hope that the church at Rome will support him in taking it to the unreached people of Spain (Romans 15:24, 28).

WEEK 1: ROMANS OVERVIEW

Begin each day this week asking God to give you insight into his righteousness, mercy, and grace.

When the church at Rome received this letter from the apostle Paul, it would have been read aloud to the entire church. There were no printing presses, so no copies would have been distributed to take home. Reading through the whole letter this week will give us a feel for what happened in the first century and also will give us an overview of what the letter is about as we notice the progression of Paul's arguments and repeated themes throughout.

DAY 1

Pray, then read Romans 1–4.

👁 1. Write down any repeated words, phrases, or ideas that you notice:

✦ 2. What do you learn about Paul in these chapters?

✦ 3. What do you learn about the church at Rome?

✦ 4. What do you learn about Paul's relationship with the church?

✦ 5. What do you learn about God?

♥ 6. What stands out to you from these chapters?

✦ 7. How would you briefly summarize chapters 1–4?

DAY 2

Pray, then read Romans 5–8.

👁 1. Write down any repeated words, phrases, or ideas that you notice:

✦ 2. What do you learn about Paul in these chapters?

3. What do you learn about the church at Rome?

4. What do you learn about Paul's relationship with the church?

5. What do you learn about God?

6. What stands out to you from these chapters?

7. How would you briefly summarize chapters 5–8?

Pray, then read Romans 9–11.

👁 1. Write down any repeated words, phrases, or ideas that you notice:

✦ 2. What do you learn about Paul in these chapters?

✦ 3. What do you learn about the church at Rome?

✦ 4. What do you learn about Paul's relationship with the church?

✦ 5. What do you learn about God?

💙 6. What stands out to you from these chapters?

DAY 4

Pray, then read Romans 12–16.

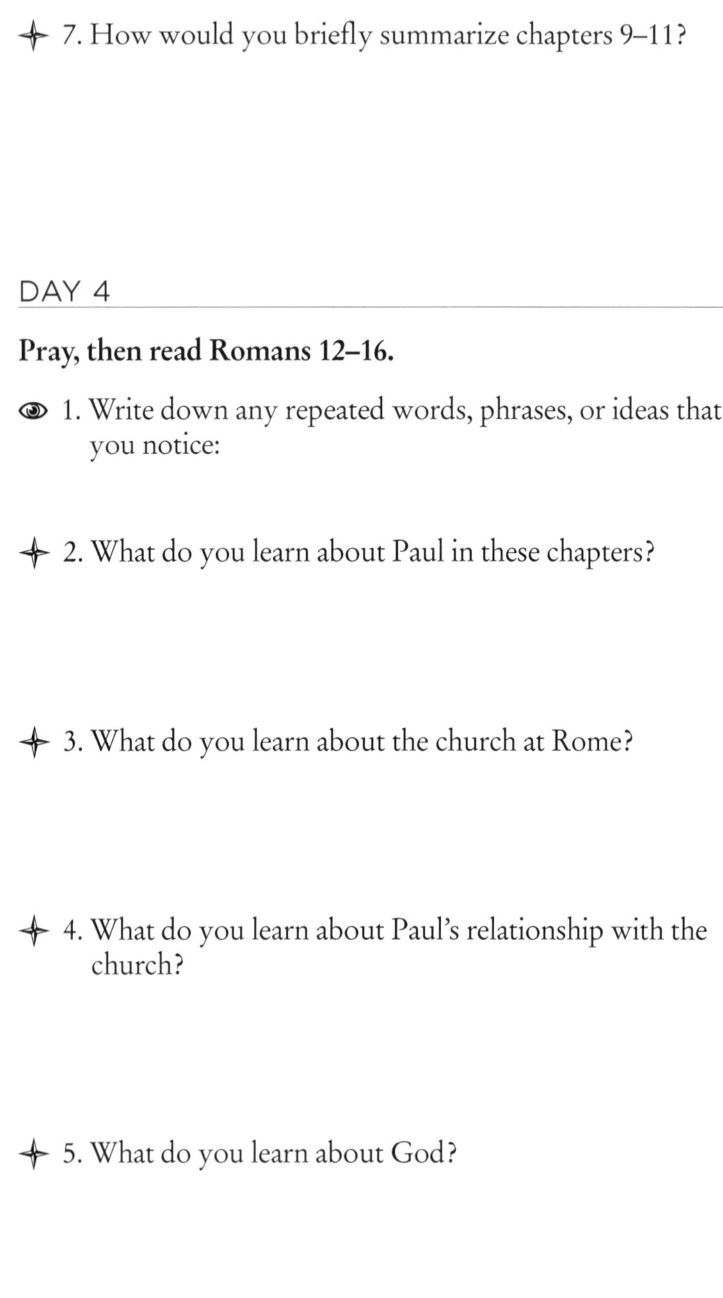

6. What stands out to you from these chapters?

7. How would you briefly summarize chapters 12–16?

DAY 5

Pray, then read Romans 1:1–7, 16–17, and 15:14–16:27.

1. What is Paul's work and what are his goals?

2. What words and phrases do you see in Romans 1:1–7 that are repeated in 16:25–27?

3. What is Paul's hope for his visit to the church in Rome?

✦ 4. You've now read through all of Romans. Why did Paul
write this letter to the church at Rome? What was his
purpose?

✦ 5. How is Romans 1:16–17 a theme for the whole book?

♥ 6. Romans is a letter power–packed with theology that
encourages church unity and gospel proclamation to all
nations for the glory of God. What do you hope to gain
from studying Romans?

WEEK 2: ROMANS 1:1-7

Pray this week for a deeper understanding of the gospel of God.

DAY 1

Pray, then read Romans 1:1–16.

Romans 1:1–2

◉ 1. Who wrote this letter?

◉ 2. How does he describe himself?

◉ 3. What was Paul called to be, and what was he set apart for?

✦ 4. What is an apostle? See Acts 1:21–26; 1 Corinthians 9:1
  and Galatians 1:1.

✦ 5. Notice the words "called" and "set apart." What is Paul
  referring to? See Acts 9:1–22. See also 1 Corinthians
  15:8–11 and Galatians 1:11–17.

6. How does this calling give authority to the words Paul writes?

7. Paul was "set apart for the gospel of God." What is the gospel of God? See Romans 1:16–17 and 3:23–26.

8. Who promised this gospel and through whom was it promised?

9. What is the significance of this gospel being promised beforehand? Why is this important for Paul to point out?

10. Where can we find these promises?

11. Read Isaiah 52:3–10 where the gospel—the good news— is promised. From where does salvation come?

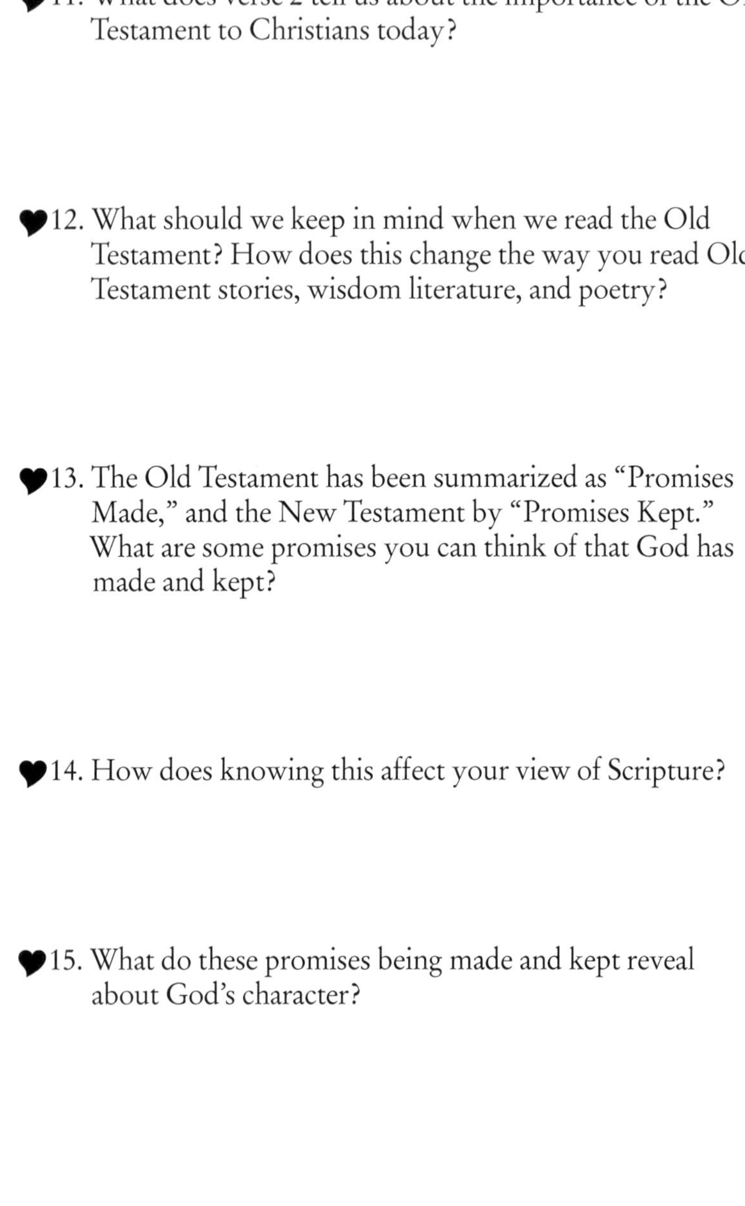

11. What does verse 2 tell us about the importance of the Old Testament to Christians today?

12. What should we keep in mind when we read the Old Testament? How does this change the way you read Old Testament stories, wisdom literature, and poetry?

13. The Old Testament has been summarized as "Promises Made," and the New Testament by "Promises Kept." What are some promises you can think of that God has made and kept?

14. How does knowing this affect your view of Scripture?

15. What do these promises being made and kept reveal about God's character?

Pray, then read Romans 1:1–7.

Romans 1:3

👁 1. With whom is the gospel of God concerned?

👁 2. Who is his Son? See the end of verse 4.

👁 3. From whom was Jesus descended?

👁 4. According to what?

✦ 5. Who was David and why would Paul emphasize that Jesus was descended from him? Read 2 Samuel 7:8–16. See also Psalm 89:35–37, 132:11–12; Jeremiah 23:5–6 and Ezekiel 34:22–24.

✦ 6. Why would Paul include the phrase "according to the flesh" after "descended from David"? What is he emphasizing with that phrase? What do we know about the Son by way of contrast with that phrase?

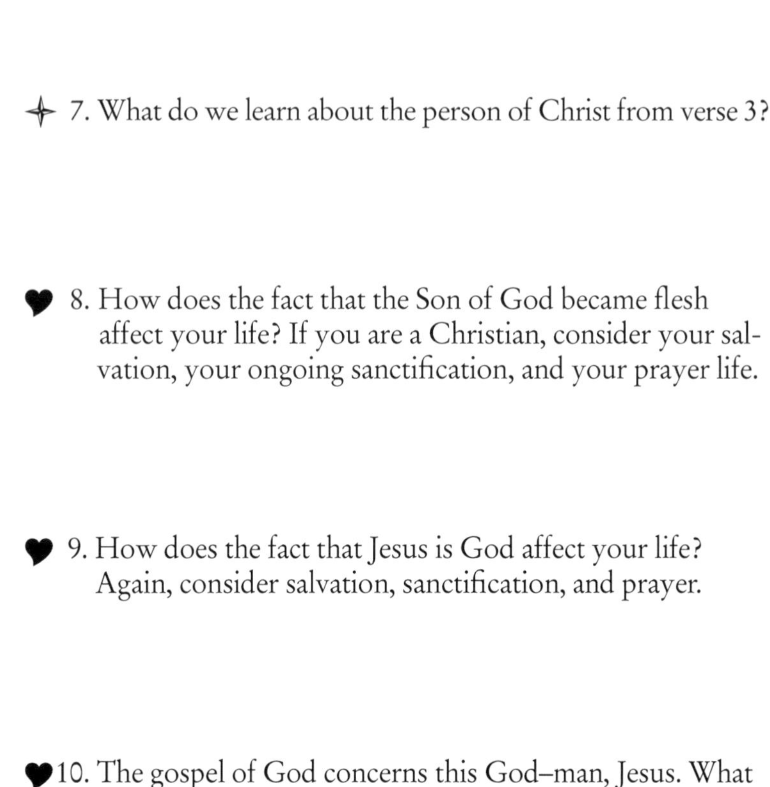

✦ 7. What do we learn about the person of Christ from verse 3?

♥ 8. How does the fact that the Son of God became flesh affect your life? If you are a Christian, consider your salvation, your ongoing sanctification, and your prayer life.

♥ 9. How does the fact that Jesus is God affect your life? Again, consider salvation, sanctification, and prayer.

♥10. The gospel of God concerns this God–man, Jesus. What other concerns can tend to displace Jesus and the gospel from the center of your life? What can churches tend to be concerned with other than Jesus and the gospel of God?

♥11. How can we make sure to keep the true gospel of God, concerning his Son, at the center of our lives?

12. How can churches make sure to keep the true gospel of God central?

Pray, then read Romans 1:1–16.

Romans 1:4

1. Who was Jesus declared to be?

2. In what and according to whom was this declaration made?

3. By what was this declaration made?

4. What does this tell us about the Spirit and his involvement in Jesus's resurrection from the dead?

5. What does "Spirit of holiness" mean, and why would Paul call the Holy Spirit the "Spirit of holiness" here?

✦ 6. The Son of God came into the world, veiled himself in weak flesh, and died a sinner's death. But he was raised in power and definitively declared to be the "Son of God" Jesus Christ our Lord. The word for "declared" could also be translated "appointed." How or in what way did the resurrection declare Jesus to be the Son of God? See Psalm 2 and Acts 2:32–36.

♥ 7. Some religions deny that Jesus is the Son of God but the apostle Paul is clearly emphasizing it in these verses. Why is that truth a vital part of the Christian message?

♥ 8. How does it encourage you to know that Jesus is God and king? He now sits on the throne ruling the nations (Psalm 2). How does it challenge you?

♥ 9. How would you use the resurrection to declare to others that Jesus is the Son of God and the ruler of all nations?

10. The power of the Holy Spirit is on display in the resurrection. In what ways do you see the power of the Holy Spirit at work in your life? See Ephesians 1:16–20.

11. Take some time to pray for the Spirit of holiness to powerfully work in you to help you have hope, fight sin, and obey the King.

DAY 4

Pray, then read Romans 1:1–7.

Romans 1:5–6

1. What has Paul received through Jesus Christ?

2. Who is included in the "we" in verse 5?

3. What is the "grace and apostleship" that Paul and others received for?

4. For whose sake? What is "his name"?

◉ 5. How widespread is the obedience of faith to be?

◉ 6. Who is included?

✦ 7. How did Paul and the other apostles receive grace and apostleship through Jesus Christ? What does Paul mean and how are grace and apostleship connected?

✦ 8. Paul tells the Roman Christians elsewhere that we are "justified by faith apart from works of the law" (3:23). What does Paul mean by "the obedience of faith"? How are obedience and faith related?

✦ 9. How does the obedience of faith, particularly among all nations, lead to the exaltation of the name of Jesus?

✦10. What does it mean to be "called to belong to Jesus Christ"?

✦11. How does belonging to Jesus Christ relate to the obedience of faith?

✦12. How would you summarize the apostles' mission? How
does this relate to the goal of this letter?

♥13. Do you belong to Jesus Christ? If so, how would you
describe the obedience of faith in your life?

♥14. How is the obedience of faith in your life for the sake of
Christ's name? How are you exalting Christ?

DAY 5

Pray, then read Romans 1:1–16.

Romans 1:7

👁 1. To whom has Paul written this letter?

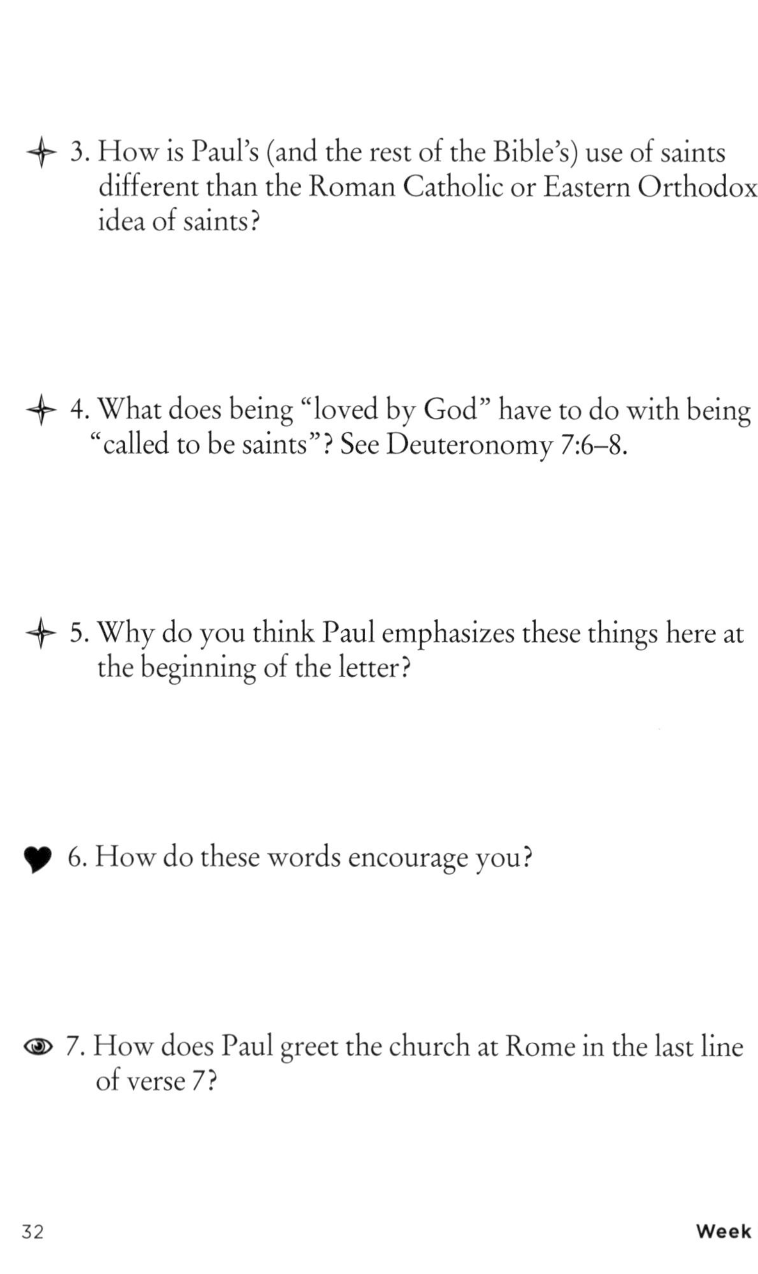

✦ 2. The word "saints" means "holy ones." Who is Paul calling holy ones?

✦ 3. How is Paul's (and the rest of the Bible's) use of saints different than the Roman Catholic or Eastern Orthodox idea of saints?

✦ 4. What does being "loved by God" have to do with being "called to be saints"? See Deuteronomy 7:6–8.

✦ 5. Why do you think Paul emphasizes these things here at the beginning of the letter?

♥ 6. How do these words encourage you?

👁 7. How does Paul greet the church at Rome in the last line of verse 7?

**Week 2

✦ 8. Grace means a gift that is not earned or deserved. Peace is
when two or more parties are reconciled to one another.
How are grace and peace related to each other? What do
you think it means for grace and peace to come "from
God our Father and the Lord Jesus Christ"?

✦ 9. In what way does Paul's letter itself impart "grace and
peace from God our Father and the Lord Jesus Christ"?

✦10. How would you sum up the first seven verses of
Romans?

WEEK 3: ROMANS 1:8–17

Praise God this week for the gospel, "the power of God for salvation to everyone who believes." Pray to be unashamed of this gospel and eager to tell it to others.

DAY 1

Pray, then read Romans 1:1–17.

Romans 1:8–12

1. Through whom and for whom does Paul thank God?

2. Why does Paul thank God for the saints in Rome?

3. What does Paul mean when he writes that their "faith is proclaimed in all the world"? (Think about the centrality of Rome to the Greco–Roman world and consider the divide between Jews and Gentiles. Christianity began in Jerusalem among the Jews.)

4. Paul had not yet traveled to Rome. Why would he thank God for their faith being proclaimed even though it wasn't the direct fruit of his ministry?

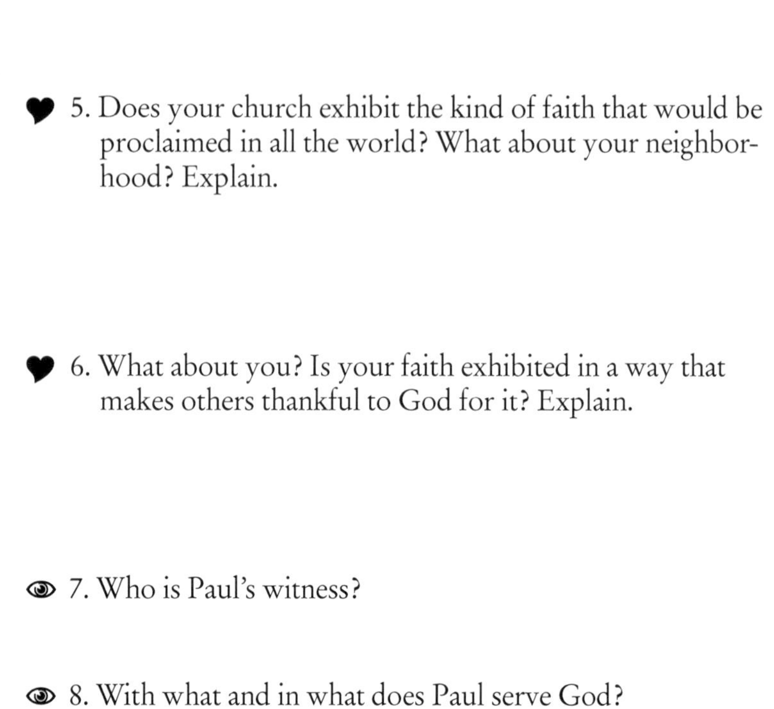

♥ 5. Does your church exhibit the kind of faith that would be proclaimed in all the world? What about your neighborhood? Explain.

♥ 6. What about you? Is your faith exhibited in a way that makes others thankful to God for it? Explain.

👁 7. Who is Paul's witness?

👁 8. With what and in what does Paul serve God?

✦ 9. What does Paul mean when he writes that he serves God with his spirit? What is he suggesting about his life and the gospel of God's Son?

👁10. How does Paul pray and what does he pray for?

👁11. What reason does Paul give in verse 11 for wanting to go to the saints at Rome?

13. What hope does Paul express in verse 12?

12. What spiritual gift would Paul have to strengthen the saints? What is he referring to?

14. Re–read verses 8–12. What is Paul's tone in these verses?

15. Sum up Paul's desire expressed in these verses and explain what you think motivates him.

16. Think about your own prayer life. Who do you pray for and what is your desire for them?

17. Paul was an apostle and, as such, he had revelation from God to impart to the saints. We are not apostles, but we can encourage the faith of our brothers and sisters in Christ. How do you seek to encourage others in your church and how have they encouraged you?

♥16. It's encouraging to know that even today we can be strengthened by Paul's spiritual gifts of apostleship and teaching. Take some time to pray to be strengthened and encouraged through studying Paul's letter to the Romans.

DAY 2

Pray, then read Romans 1:8–17.

Romans 1:13–15

👁 1. How does Paul address those in the Roman church?

👁 2. What does he want these brothers to know?

👁 3. Why hasn't Paul previously visited Rome?

👁 4. Why has he wanted to visit these brothers?

✦ 5. What harvest has he previously reaped "among the rest of the Gentiles"?

✦ 6. What kind of harvest does Paul want to reap among the Romans?

7. To whom is Paul under obligation?

8. What is the obligation? See Acts 9:15–16 and 1 Corinthians 9:16.

9. What do these categories of Greeks and barbarians and wise and foolish suggest about whom the gospel is for?

10. What is Paul eager to do?

11. Paul is eager to preach the gospel to those he's writing to in Rome, but they are Christians. Why would Paul think it's important for him to preach the gospel among Christians?

12. Does this expand your answer to what Paul means by reaping a harvest among them?

♥ 13. Do you think of yourself as needing the gospel preached to you? If you're a believer, why do you still need to regularly hear the gospel?

♥ 14. What are some of the ways the gospel applies to your daily life?

♥ 15. When authorities questioned Peter and John, they responded, "We cannot but speak of what we have seen and heard." Are you like Paul, Peter, and John, eager to speak the gospel to others? What were the circumstances the last time you shared the gospel with an unbeliever or spoke of the gospel with another believer?

DAY 3

Pray, then read Romans 1:8–17.

Romans 1:16

👁 1. Of what is Paul not ashamed?

✦ 2. How does this statement connect to the previous verses? (Why does this statement begin with "For"?)

◉ 3. What is the gospel?

◉ 4. What word tells us whom the gospel is for?

◉ 5. What must one do for salvation? See also John 6:29.

◉ 6. What is the order in which the gospel goes out?

✦ 7. What does Paul mean when he writes that the gospel "is
the power of God for salvation"?

✦ 8. What does belief have to do with it?

✦ 9. What is salvation? What are believers saved from? See
Romans 1:18.

♥ 10. Have you experienced the saving power of the gospel? If
so, describe your experience.

♥11. Have you ever been ashamed of the gospel? What do you think you are mistaken about or fearful of in those times when you are reluctant to share with others?

♥12. Why should we not allow shame to cause us to water down or add to the gospel?

♥13. How does verse 16 give you confidence to share the gospel clearly with "everyone"?

DAY 4

Pray, then read Romans 1:8–17.

Romans 1:17

✦ 1. How does the "For" connect verse 17 to verse 16?

✦ 2. What does "it" refer to?

◉ 3. What is revealed in the gospel?

✦ 4. Read Romans 3:21–26 and 10:4–8. What does the "righteousness of God" mean? What has been revealed?

◉ 5. This righteousness of God is "from" and "for" what?

✦ 6. What is "faith"? To what word in verse 16 does it correspond? See also Romans 4:5, 20–25 and 10:9–11.

✦ 7. What does it mean that the righteousness of God is revealed "from faith for faith"? What is Paul trying to convey about "the righteousness of God" that is revealed in the gospel?

◉ 8. What is written? (Quoted from Habakkuk 2:4.)

✦ 9. What does "The righteous shall live by faith" mean? See Habakkuk 2:2–5.

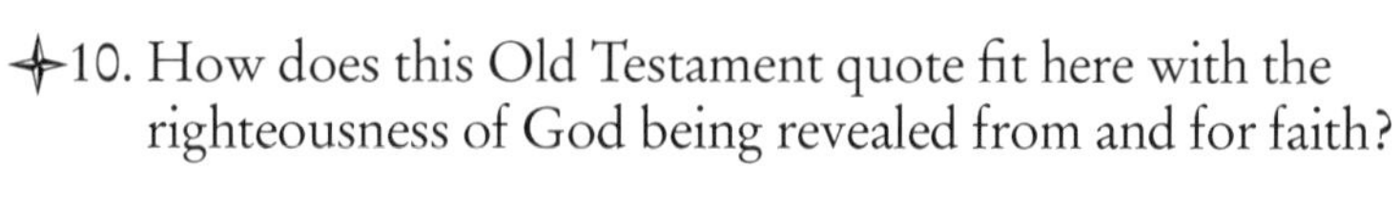

✦10. How does this Old Testament quote fit here with the righteousness of God being revealed from and for faith?

✦11. How would you explain verse 17 to a friend?

♥12. What does it mean for your life that the righteousness of God is revealed in the gospel?

♥13. Can you say that you live by faith? How does your life show this?

DAY 5

Pray, then read Romans 1:1–17.

Romans 1:8–17

✦ 1. In verses 8–17, we read of Paul's eagerness to preach the gospel. Why is the gospel such good news?

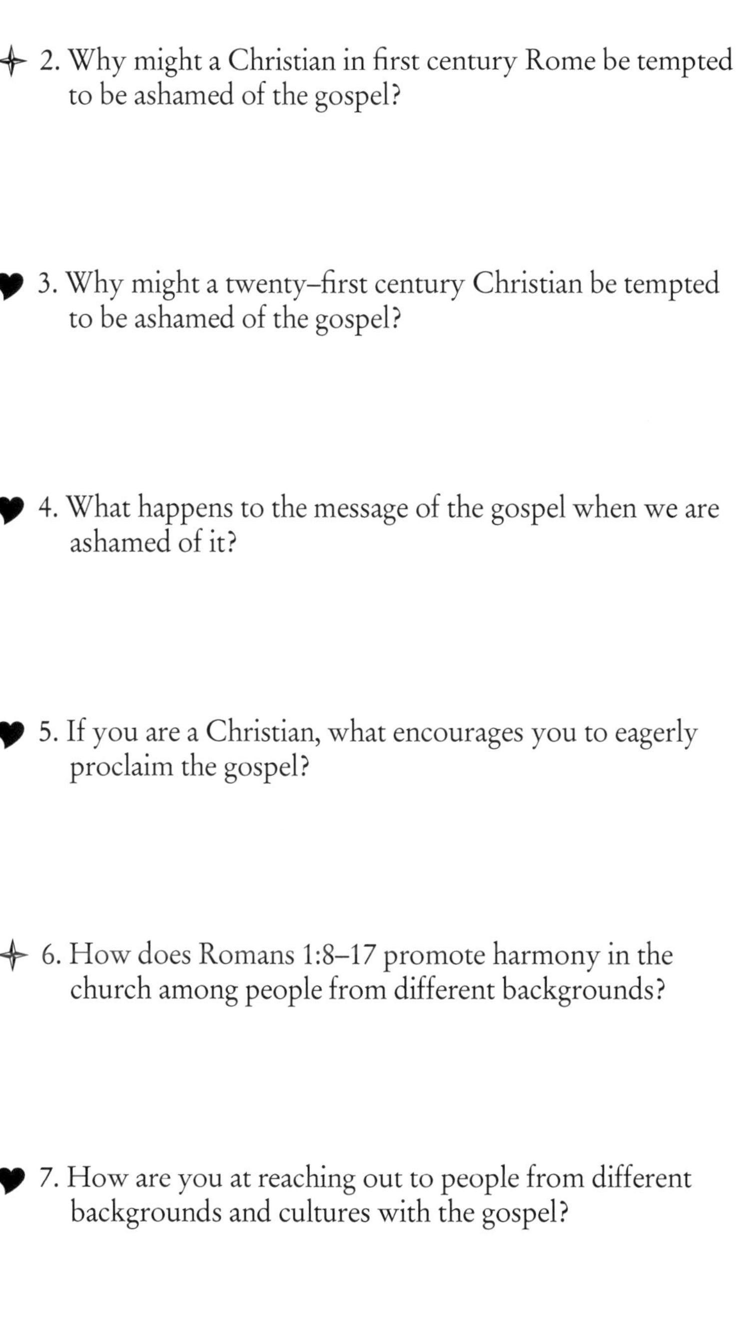

2. Why might a Christian in first century Rome be tempted to be ashamed of the gospel?

3. Why might a twenty–first century Christian be tempted to be ashamed of the gospel?

4. What happens to the message of the gospel when we are ashamed of it?

5. If you are a Christian, what encourages you to eagerly proclaim the gospel?

6. How does Romans 1:8–17 promote harmony in the church among people from different backgrounds?

7. How are you at reaching out to people from different backgrounds and cultures with the gospel?

♥ 8. Have you ever attended a church that seemed to be ashamed of the gospel? In what ways might a local church water down the gospel to make it more palatable to people?

♥ 9. What are the implications of Romans 1:8–17 for local churches? Think about the preaching, singing, liturgy, and order of service.

♥ 10. Romans 1:16–17 is the theme of Paul's letter to the Romans. Paul is unashamed to preach the gospel because it is the power of God to save sinners. In it the righteousness of God is revealed by faith. The rest of Romans will unpack this glorious gospel. Take some time to praise God for this spectacularly good news.

WEEK 4: ROMANS 1:18–32

Pray this week to have a thankful heart, to acknowledge God as
God, and to point others to the eternal power and divine nature
of God.

Pray, then read Romans 1:16–32.

Romans 1:18–20

◉ 1. What is revealed and from where?

◉ 2. What is the wrath of God against?

◉ 3. What do men do? And how do they do it?

✦ 4. What is the "wrath of God"?

✦ 5. Verse 18 says, "the wrath of God is revealed from heav-
en." In the context of the remainder of chapter 1, how
is the wrath of God being revealed in the world? (Note:
This verse is not referring to final judgment.) How do
verses 24 and following show how God's wrath is being
revealed?

✦ 6. What do "ungodliness" and "unrighteousness" mean?

✦ 7. What does the "For" in verse 18 point back to? Why does Paul bring up the wrath of God and the unrighteousness of men here?

👁 8. What is plain to unrighteous men?

👁 9. How has it been made plain?

✦10. How does the "For" in verse 19 connect it to verse 18?

👁11. What has been clearly perceived?

👁12. Since when and in what have these invisible attributes of God been perceived?

✦13. How does the "For" of verse 20 connect with verse 19?

👁14. What does Paul conclude at the end of verse 20?

✦15. How do visible things testify to God's invisible attributes? See Psalm 19:1–6; Isaiah 6:3 and Acts 14:15–17.

♥16. What about this passage suggests that science is a worthwhile pursuit for Christians?

♥17. Have you perceived God's eternal power and divine nature in his creation? A hymn written by Stuart K. Hine sings:

> O Lord my God, when I in awesome wonder consider all the worlds Thy hands have made, I see the stars, I hear the rolling thunder, Thy pow'r throughout the universe displayed. Then sings my soul, my Savior God, to Thee: how great Thou art, how great Thou art! Then sings my soul, my Savior God, to Thee: how great Thou art, how great Thou art!

Give an example of a specific time when you felt this way:

18. If a friend told you that she thinks it would be unfair of God to condemn a person who hasn't heard the gospel, how would you use verses 18–19 to explain to her why that person is without excuse?

DAY 2

Pray, then read Romans 1:16–32.

Romans 1:21–23

1. To whom does "they" in verses 21–23 refer?

2. What did they know?

3. What did they not do?

4. How does the "For" at the beginning of verse 21 connect verse 21 to the previous verses?

5. What happens as a result of not honoring God as God or giving thanks to him?

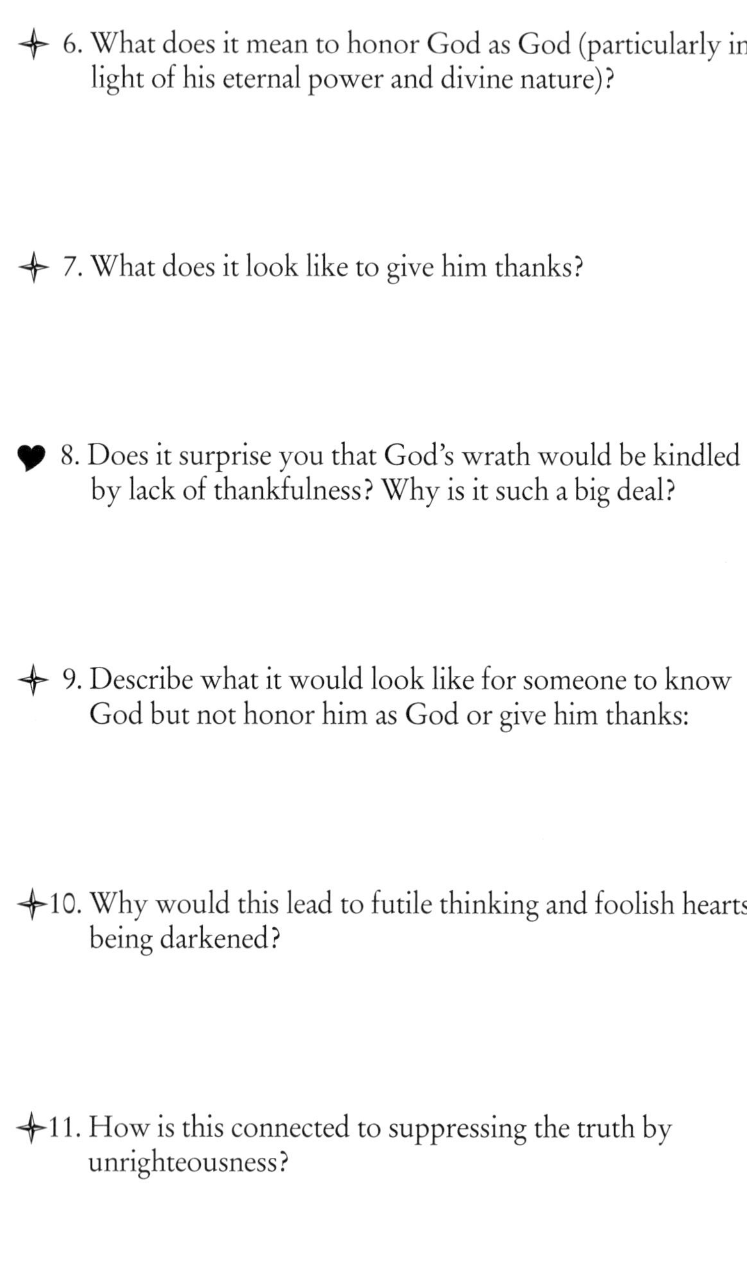

✦ 6. What does it mean to honor God as God (particularly in light of his eternal power and divine nature)?

✦ 7. What does it look like to give him thanks?

♥ 8. Does it surprise you that God's wrath would be kindled by lack of thankfulness? Why is it such a big deal?

✦ 9. Describe what it would look like for someone to know God but not honor him as God or give him thanks:

✦ 10. Why would this lead to futile thinking and foolish hearts being darkened?

✦ 11. How is this connected to suppressing the truth by unrighteousness?

12. What did they claim, and what did they become?

13. What did they exchange?

14. What does "the glory of the immortal God" mean, and how does that compare to images of created things? See also Jeremiah 2:11–13.

15. How have the major religions of the world made this exchange? Consider Hinduism, Buddhism, Islam, Humanism, and even some Christian traditions.

16. How is this foolish and dark?

17. In our verses today, we see how vital it is to honor God as God and give him thanks. This is worship. Is your life characterized by thankfulness or complaining? How can you increase your thankfulness?

♥18. How do verses 18–23 inform our evangelism?

DAY 3

Pray, then read Romans 1:16–32.

Romans 1:24–25

✦ 1. What is "therefore" there for? How are verses 24–25 connected to the previous verses?

✦ 2. To whom do the "them" and the "they" in verses 24–25 refer?

👁 3. What did these men have in their hearts?

👁 4. What did God do?

✦ 5. What does it mean that God "gave them up" to impurity and the dishonoring of their bodies?

✦ 6. What does "impurity" mean?

✦ 7. What do you think Paul is referring to when he writes,
    "the dishonoring of their bodies among themselves"?
    What kind of sin is this?

👁 8. Why did God give these men up to impurity and the
    dishonoring of their bodies?

✦ 9. What does this have to do with the idolatry described in
    verses 22–23?

✦10. Notice verse 25 is basically a restatement of verses 22–23.
    How is idolatry the same as exchanging the truth about
    God for a lie? See Isaiah 44:6–20.

❤11. Today, western cultures don't generally have idols that can be seen with the eye. But such cultures still exchange the truth about God for a lie and worship and serve things that are not God. What are some of the idols that are worshipped in your culture?

❤12. Which of these idols are most tempting to you?

❤13. In your culture, how do you see idols leading people to impurity and the dishonoring of their bodies among themselves?

❤14. How do you guard your heart against idolatry?

DAY 4

Pray, then read Romans 1:16–32.

Romans 1:26–27

👁 1. What did God give men up to?

✦ 2. For what reason did God give them up? To what in the
previous verses is Paul referring?

👁 3. What dishonorable passions does Paul describe?

✦ 4. What kind of behavior is Paul describing in these verses?

👁 5. What does Paul call the acts these men commit, and what
do they receive for their error?

✦ 6. How do western cultures today see homosexuality?

✦ 7. What is God's position on homosexuality? Does being
in love justify homosexual behavior or is the desire itself
distorted? See also Leviticus 18:22 and 20:13.

✦ 8. What does it mean that men receive "in themselves the due penalty for their error"? See also 1 Corinthians 6:18–20.

✦ 9. Why do you think Paul focuses on sexual sin here? What makes it idolatrous? What does it have to do with the created order? See Genesis 1:26–28 and 2:18–25.

♥ 10. Do you struggle with sexual sin? Reread verses 16–17. That same gospel power can work in you to overcome this sin. Look to Jesus! He is the righteousness of God. The more beautiful he becomes to you, the less hold lust will have over you. Sexual sin is powerful. Get help from someone in your church to fight this sin by looking to Jesus.

♥ 11. How can we as sisters in Christ help other church members who struggle with sexual sin?

Pray, then read Romans 1:16–32.

Romans 1:28–32

👁 1. What phrase is repeated for the third time in verse 28?

👁 2. What did God give them up to?

👁 3. Why did God give them up?

👁 4. With what were these people, who did not acknowledge God, filled?

👁 5. What are they full of?

👁 6. What are they?

❤ 7. Does anything on these three lists surprise you? Does it surprise you that being a gossip or being disobedient to parents are on the same list as haters of God and ruthless?

✦ 8. What does it tell you that these things we often excuse as normal or minor are on the list?

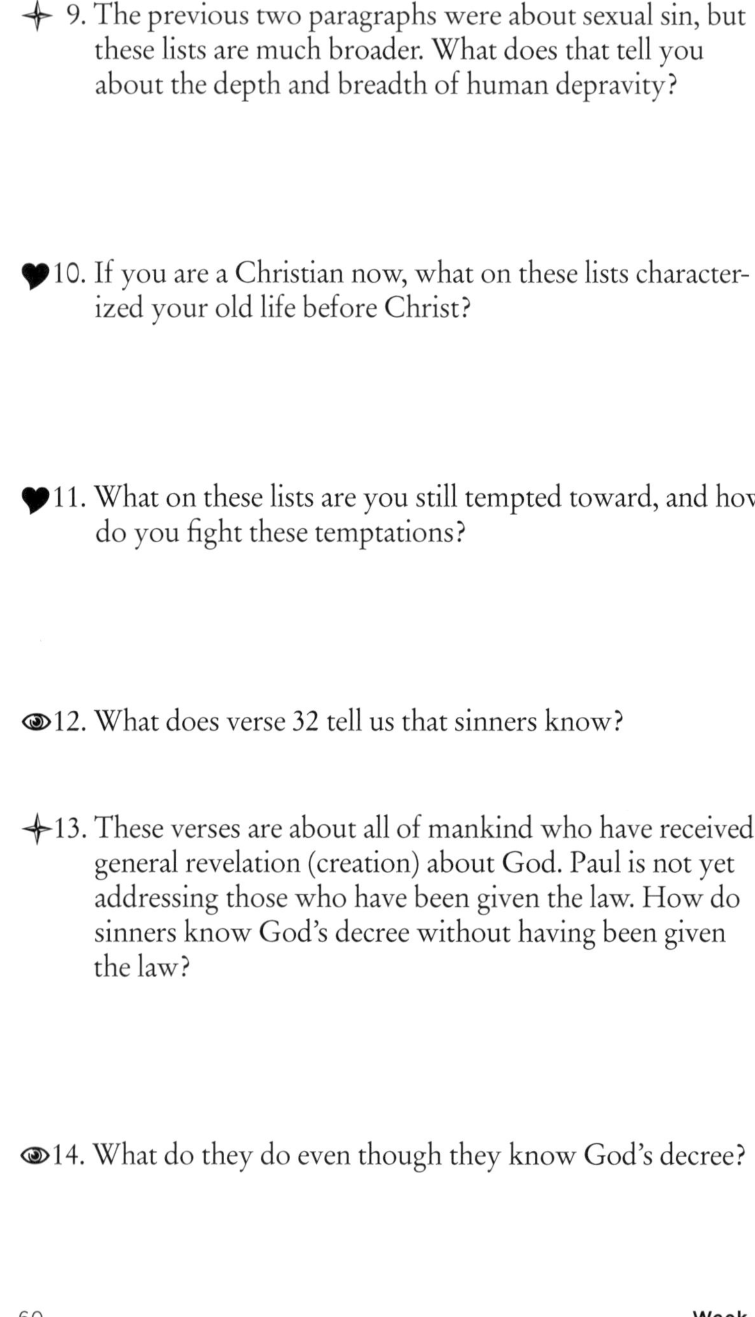

✦ 9. The previous two paragraphs were about sexual sin, but these lists are much broader. What does that tell you about the depth and breadth of human depravity?

♥10. If you are a Christian now, what on these lists character-ized your old life before Christ?

♥11. What on these lists are you still tempted toward, and how do you fight these temptations?

👁12. What does verse 32 tell us that sinners know?

✦13. These verses are about all of mankind who have received general revelation (creation) about God. Paul is not yet addressing those who have been given the law. How do sinners know God's decree without having been given the law?

👁14. What do they do even though they know God's decree?

15. How does this show a greater depth of evil?

16. What examples have you seen in today's culture of people
    who not only do evil things but give approval to those
    who practice them?

17. Have you ever given this kind of approval?

18. If you are a Christian, give God praise for delivering you
    from being filled with sin!

19. Write a short summary of Paul's main point in verses
    18–32. What does Paul want his readers to understand
    from these verses?

✦20. Notice that Paul repeats, "God gave them up," three times. What does the rampant immorality of the world have to do with God's wrath?

♥21. What is the only hope for the world? See Romans 1:16–17.

NOTES

WEEK 5: ROMANS 2

This week, pray to feel the weight of the truth that no one has an excuse for sin, and pray to understand what it means to have a circumcised heart that leads you to be patient in well–doing, to seek after God, and not to be self–seeking and disobedient.

DAY 1

Pray, then read Romans 1:18–2:11.

Romans 2:1–5

👁 1. Who has no excuse?

👁 2. What does a man who passes judgment on others do?

👁 3. Why does the man who judges another condemn himself?

👁 4. What do we know about the judgment of God?

✦ 5. What does the word "things" in verses 1, 2, and 3 refer to? Are these the same "things" referred to in 1:32?

👁 6. What question does Paul ask in verse 3?

✦ 7. Why does Paul ask this question, and how would he
answer it?

✦ 8. What is God condemning: men judging others or men
doing evil deeds and judging others for those same evil
deeds? Explain:

◉ 9. In Paul's next question, what does he suggest that his
readers presume upon when they practice the same sins
they judge?

✦10. How is doing these things presuming upon God's kindness, forbearance and patience?

◉11. What is God's kindness meant to do?

✦12. Why doesn't God immediately punish "gossips, slander-
ers, haters of God, insolent, haughty, boastful, inventors
of evil, disobedient to parents, foolish, faithless, heartless,
ruthless"? (Verse 32 says they deserve to die.)

👁13. Why don't men repent?

👁14. What is the result of their hard and impenitent hearts?

👁15. What will happen on the day of wrath?

✦16. Summarize verses 1–5 in your own words. What argument is Paul making?

✦17. Notice verse 1 starts with a "therefore." How is Paul's argument in verses 1–5 connected to his argument in 1:18–32? See Week 4, Day 5, Question 19 for your summary of verses 18–32.

♥18. Some people argue that truth is relative and that therefore we cannot claim that someone's behavior is wrong if it feels right to him or her. How could you use verses 1–5 to show that deep down all people have absolute standards of right and wrong?

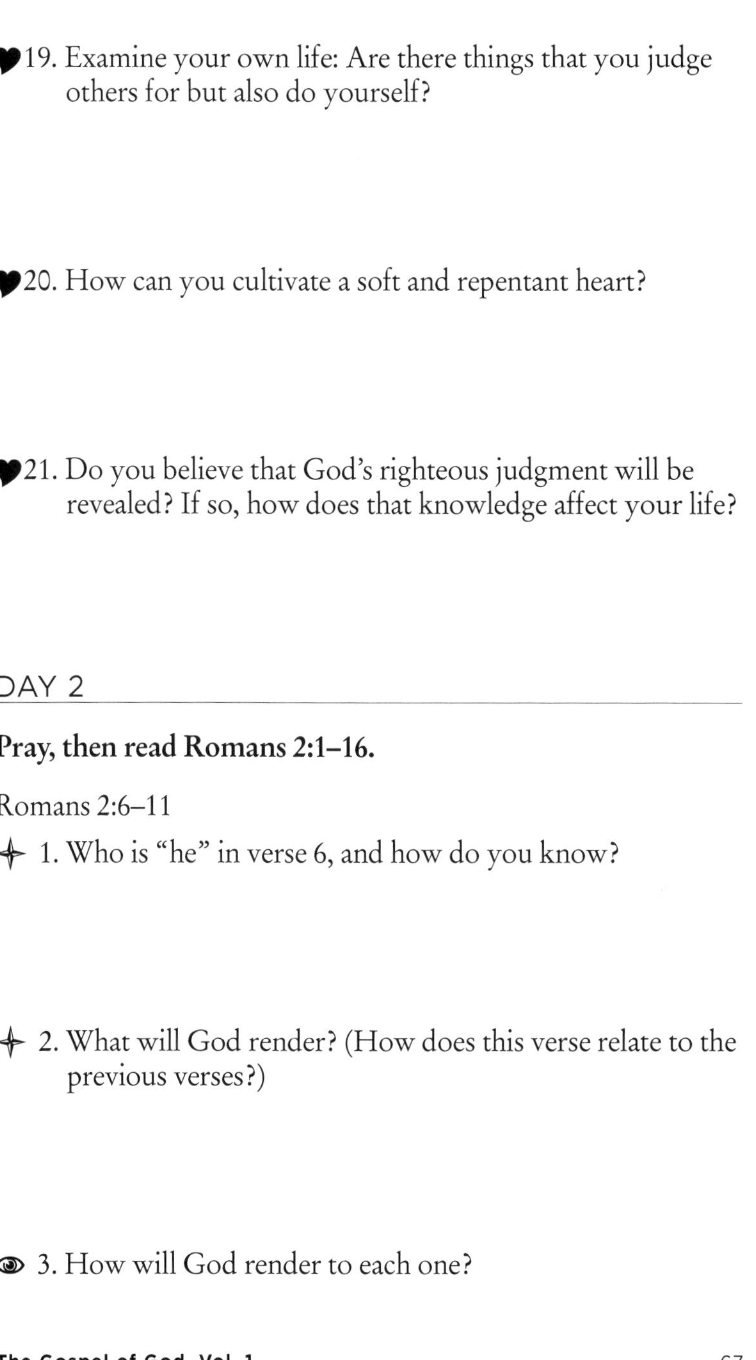

19. Examine your own life: Are there things that you judge others for but also do yourself?

20. How can you cultivate a soft and repentant heart?

21. Do you believe that God's righteous judgment will be revealed? If so, how does that knowledge affect your life?

DAY 2

Pray, then read Romans 2:1–16.

Romans 2:6–11

1. Who is "he" in verse 6, and how do you know?

2. What will God render? (How does this verse relate to the previous verses?)

3. How will God render to each one?

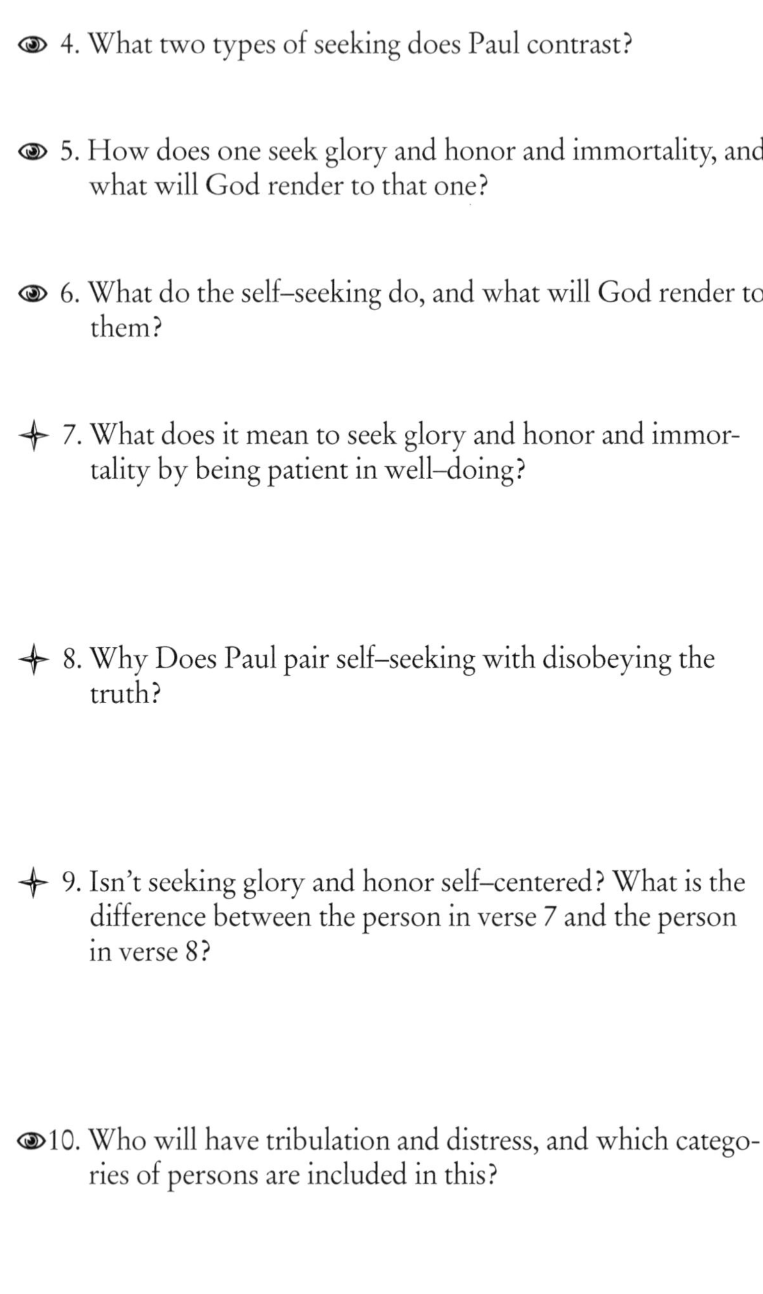

4. What two types of seeking does Paul contrast?

5. How does one seek glory and honor and immortality, and what will God render to that one?

6. What do the self–seeking do, and what will God render to them?

7. What does it mean to seek glory and honor and immortality by being patient in well–doing?

8. Why Does Paul pair self–seeking with disobeying the truth?

9. Isn't seeking glory and honor self–centered? What is the difference between the person in verse 7 and the person in verse 8?

10. Who will have tribulation and distress, and which categories of persons are included in this?

⊙11. What will everyone who does good have, and what categories of persons are included in this?

⊙12. What follows from Paul's statements about how God will
render judgment? (Notice the "For" at the beginning of
verse 11.)

✦13. Paul repeats "to the Jew first and also the Greek" from
1:16. Looking at 1:16 and 2:9–10 together, what is Paul
saying about Jew and Greeks? (What's he saying about all
of humankind?) How are they alike?

✦14. How are verses 6 and 11 related?

✦15. Does it surprise you that the Bible teaches that God will
render judgment according to people's works—whether
they do good or evil? Aren't we saved by grace through
faith alone, not according to works? See Romans 1:16–17;
Ephesians 2:8–10, James 2:14–26 and Revelation 20:11–15
and explain your answer:

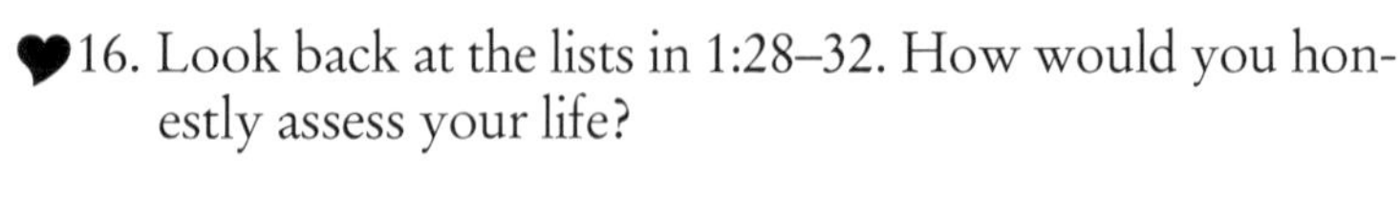

16. Look back at the lists in 1:28–32. How would you honestly assess your life?

17. How would you apply 1:16–17 to this assessment?

DAY 3

Pray, then read Romans 2:6–29.

Romans 2:12–16

1. What will happen to "all who have sinned without the law," and what will happen to "all who have sinned under the law"?

2. Paul begins verse 12 with a "For." What does this have to do with the previous verses?

3. Who are those who have sinned without the law and who are those who have sinned under the law? What groups of people is Paul referring to?

4. Who is not automatically considered righteous before God, and who will be justified?

5. The phrase "who will be justified" is future tense and speaks of a final justification. Explain why verse 13 does not contradict 3:20. (See also James 2:14–26.)

6. When are Gentiles who "do not have the law" a law to themselves?

7. What does this show?

8. What is the result of the work of the law being written on their hearts?

9. According to Paul's gospel, on what day will this happen?

10. What does it mean for "the work of the law" to be written on a person's heart?

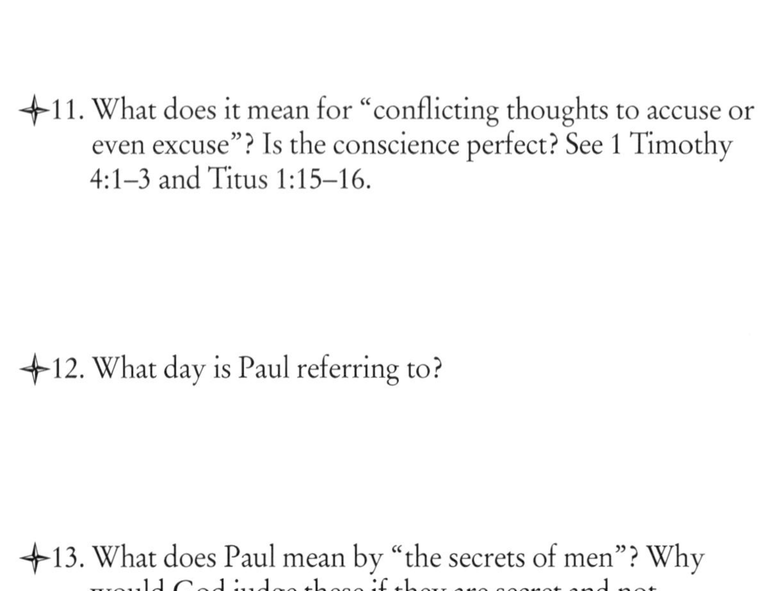

✦11. What does it mean for "conflicting thoughts to accuse or even excuse"? Is the conscience perfect? See 1 Timothy 4:1–3 and Titus 1:15–16.

✦12. What day is Paul referring to?

✦13. What does Paul mean by "the secrets of men"? Why would God judge these if they are secret and not outward?

✦14. While God did not give the Gentiles a written law, he did give them a conscience, the work of the law written on their hearts. How does this make Gentiles accountable before God?

✦15. Sum up Paul's argument in verses 12–16 in your own words:

16. If a friend told you that she thinks it would be unfair for God to judge a person who had never heard about the true God, how would you use Paul's argument from these verses to respond?

17. If all who have sinned, without the law or under the law, will perish, what is the only hope for sinners?

DAY 4

Pray, then read Romans 2:12–29.

Romans 2:17–24

1. Who is Paul specifically addressing in these verses?

2. What does the Jew do and know?

3. Why does he do it?

4. What is he sure of?

5. What does he have in the law?

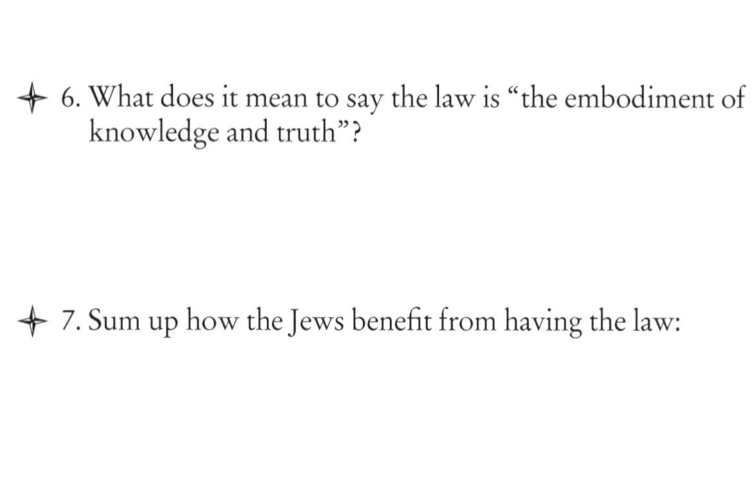

✦ 6. What does it mean to say the law is "the embodiment of knowledge and truth"?

✦ 7. Sum up how the Jews benefit from having the law:

👁 8. What does Paul ask at the beginning of verse 21?

👁 9. Paul then asks a series of questions in verses 21–22. What sins does he specifically point out?

👁10. What do these Jews who boast in the law do?

👁11. What is written?

✦12. Read Ezekiel 36:16–23. How did the Jews profane the name of the Lord when they were scattered among the nations? (Consider why the people were scattered.)

✦13. Sum up how the Jews of Paul's time were dishonoring God:

✦14. How do verses 17–24 explain why "all who have sinned under the law will be judged by the law" (v. 12)?

♥15. The church is the new people of God, both Jew and Gentile. As Christians we have the full "embodiment of knowledge and truth" in our Bibles. But possession of God's law alone is not what honors God. How can local churches be guilty of dishonoring God in the same way the Jews did?

♥16. How can individual Christians be guilty of dishonoring God?

♥17. How can local churches and individual Christians guard themselves against avoid dishonoring God?

Pray, then read Romans 2:12–29.

Romans 2:25–29

👁 1. What are the circumstances that make circumcision of value?

👁 2. What if a circumcised Jew breaks the law?

✦ 3. What is circumcision and what did it stand for? Read Genesis 17:9–14.

✦ 4. Considering the meaning of circumcision, what is Paul saying about a Jew's relationship with God if he breaks the law?

✦ 5. What does this have to do with the previous verses?

👁 6. How will the uncircumcision of man be regarded if he keeps the precepts of the law?

✦ 7. What does Paul mean by "precepts of the law"?

👁 8. What will the physically uncircumcised man who keeps the law do?

👁 9. What does not make one a Jew, and what does not constitute circumcision?

👁10. What is a true Jew, and what is true circumcision?

👁11. How does true circumcision occur and not occur?

✦12. What does Paul mean when he writes that "a Jew is one inwardly and circumcision is a matter of the heart"? Who are the Jews in relation to God?

✦13. God told the people of Israel to circumcise their hearts. Read Deuteronomy 10:12–16. What did God mean by this?

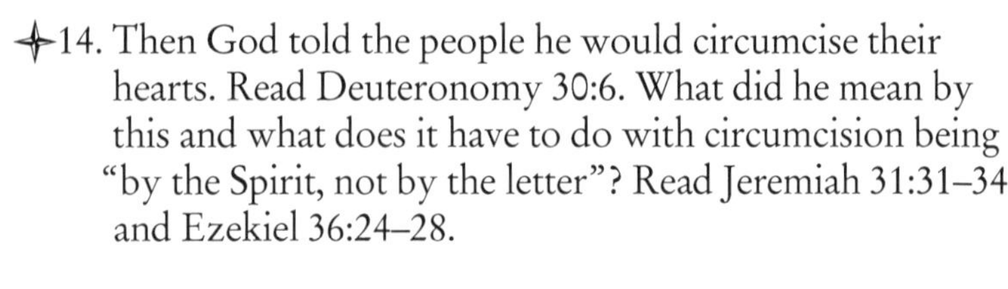

✦14. Then God told the people he would circumcise their hearts. Read Deuteronomy 30:6. What did he mean by this and what does it have to do with circumcision being "by the Spirit, not by the letter"? Read Jeremiah 31:31–34 and Ezekiel 36:24–28.

✦15. What does Jesus's death and resurrection have to do with circumcision by the Spirit? See Matthew 26:26–28; John 16:5–15 and Hebrews 10:19–22.

♥16. Has your heart been circumcised? Has the Spirit written God's law on your heart? If so, meditate on God's goodness and rejoice!

♥17. If your heart has been circumcised, you are a member of the people of God. How does this play out for you in your local church?

👁18. From where does the praise of the man with the circumcised heart come?

✦19. Why would Paul end this section contrasting the praise of man with the praise of God?

♥20. In what ways are you tempted to go after the praise of men and how does gaining the praise of God help you resist those temptations?

✦21. Look back through your notes from this week, specifically the summaries on Day 1, Question 16; Day 2, Question 13; Day 3, Question 15; and Day 4, Questions 13 and 14. Putting these together with what you've studied today, summarize Paul's argument in chapter 2:

✦22. Why is Paul writing this to believers in the church at Rome? (Think about the purpose of this letter.)

♥23. Why is this message important to us today?

WEEK 6: ROMANS 3:1-20

Pray this week to know the depths of your sin and the impossibility of being justified by works in God's sight.

DAY 1

Pray, then read Romans 2:17–3:20.

Romans 3:1–4

👁 1. What questions does Paul ask?

✚ 2. Why does Paul ask these questions here in the letter?

👁 3. What are the answers to the questions?

✚ 4. What are "the oracles of God" and what does it mean that the Jews ere entrusted with them? (You might want to look up *oracle* in a dictionary.)

✚ 5. How would this be a benefit to the Jews?

👁 6. What does Paul ask about some of the Jews' faithlessness?

✦ 7. How were some of the Jews unfaithful? (Can you think
of some examples from Old Testament history?)

◉ 8. In what emphatic way does Paul answer his own
question?

✦ 9. Why does he answer this way? How was God showing his faithfulness to the Jews of Paul's day, and what
do the oracles of God have to do with his continuing
faithfulness?

◉10. What does Paul write about God's character?

◉11. Paul then quotes from Psalm 51:4. Write out the quote.
(Note that Paul is using the Greek translation of the
Hebrew Old Testament (LXX) when he quotes the
Psalm. Though the wording is a little different, the mean-
ing is the same.):

✦12. Read Psalm 51:1–5. What is the great King David doing in this Psalm?

✦13. So what is Paul arguing in verses 3–4?

♥14. The Jews were God's chosen people, his treasured possession, but they were unfaithful to their God. Still God remains faithful to his promise. If you were a Jew, how would this have given you hope for yourself and your loved ones?

♥15. In the New Testament, the church is called God's chosen, "a people for his own possession" (1 Peter 2:9). How does God's faithfulness to the Jews give hope to us in the church?

♥16. How does God's faithfulness spur you on to remain faithful to him?

♥17. Even with the oracles of God, some Jews were unfaithful. How can someone who has grown up in church and been taught the Bible be warned by verses 1–4? How can that person be encouraged by verses 1–4?

DAY 2

Pray, then read Romans 2:25–3:20.

Romans 3:5–8

👁 1. What questions does Paul ask in verse 5?

👁 2. How does he answer the questions in verse 6?

👁 3. What two questions does Paul ask in verses 7 and 8?

👁 4. From where do these questions come?

✦ 5. Sum up what Paul's opponents are arguing about him:

👁 6. What does Paul say about these opponents?

✦ 7. What is the answer to Paul's questions? If our sin shows God's righteousness, how can God judge us, inflicting his wrath on us for that sin?

✦ 8. In light of what you've studied in Romans so far, who do you think these opponents are?

✦ 9. Paul answers these arguments more fully in chapter 6. Why do you think he brings up the arguments here in the letter? (What in the previous chapters leads to addressing these arguments?)

❤ 10. What similar arguments have you heard from friends or family against the gospel of grace?

❤ 11. After hearing the gospel, a woman responded, "Your religion is so easy!" (It was during the Muslim month of fasting when they cannot eat or drink during daylight hours.) What would you say in response to this woman?

♥12. Do you believe that your unrighteousness by contrast shows the righteousness of God? Your lies highlight his truth? How would you explain to a friend why this does not encourage you to sin so that God is glorified?

DAY 3

Pray, then read Romans 3:1–20.

Romans 3:9–18

👁 1. Following verses 1–8, Paul asks: "What then? Are we Jews any better off?" How does he answer his own question?

👁 2. Why are the Jews not any better off?

✦ 3. But Paul previously argued that the Jews had the advantage of being "entrusted with the oracles of God." How is being under sin the great equalizer?

✦ 4. What does it mean to be "under sin"?

5. Writing "as it is written" in v. 10, Paul goes on to quote from a number of Psalms, a Proverb, and Isaiah. Compare Paul's quotes to their corresponding Old Testament verses and notice whom the Old Testament passages were written about. (Be sure to read the Old Testament verses in their context to understand the message the author wants to convey.)

- Romans 3:10–12 // *Psalm 14:1–3* and *Psalm 53:1–3*

   Read Psalms 14 and 53. About whom are Psalms 14:1–3 and 53:1–3 written?

   Put verses 10–12 in your own words with the Psalms in mind:

- Romans 3:13a // *Psalm 5:9*

   Read Psalm 5. About whom is Psalm 5:9 written?

   Put verse 13a in your own words with Psalm 5:9 in mind:

- Romans 3:13b // *Psalm 140:3*

  Read Psalm 140:1–3. About whom is Psalm 140:3 written?

  Put verse 13b in your own words with Psalm 140:3 in mind:

- Romans 3:14 // *Psalm 10:7*

  Read Psalm 10. About whom is Psalm 10:7 written?

  Put verse 14 in your own words with Psalm 10:7 in mind:

- Romans 3: 15 // *Proverbs 1:16*

  Read Proverbs 1:9–18. About whom is Proverbs 1:16 written?

  Put verse 15 in your own words with Proverbs 1:16 in mind:

- Romans 3:15–17 // *Isaiah 59:7–8*

  Read Isaiah 59:1–8. About whom is Isaiah 59:7–8 written?

  Put verses 15–17 in your own words with Isaiah 59:7–8 in mind:

- Romans 3:18 // *Psalm 36:1*

  Read Psalm 36. About whom is Psalm 36:1 written?

  Put verse 18 in your own words with Psalm 36:1 in mind:

✦ 6. Apart from Isaiah 59, the Old Testament passages that Paul uses are written about the wicked enemies of God's people. But Paul applies these verses to "good" religious people who consider themselves God's chosen people. What does this tell you about all of humankind?

✦ 7. What does verse 13a tell you about the heart of sinful man? See also Ephesians 2:1–3.

✦ 8. What do verses 13b–14 tell you about the words of the unrighteous?

✦ 9. What do verses 15–17 tell you?

✦10. What does fear of God have to do with these things?

♥11. Have you ever seen yourself in the way Romans 3:10–18 describes? Explain:

✦12. Paul will offer hope in Romans. The Old Testament passages we read also offer hope. Read Psalm 5:11–12. Who are the ones who rejoice and sing for joy forever? (You

may also want to read Isaiah 59:15b–21 to see God's
promise to his sinful people.)

13. Have you taken refuge in Jesus Christ and been made
alive? If so, rejoice! You are no longer in Romans 3:10–18.

14. If you have not taken refuge in Christ, your life, heart,
mouth, and feet are described in Romans 3:10–18. The
good news is that you don't have to clean yourself up.
You can't! Just as you cannot raise yourself from the dead.
Take refuge in Christ. He will cover you with favor and
give you joy forevermore.

DAY 4

Pray, then read Romans 3:9–21.

Romans 3:19–20

1. Sum up Romans 3:9–18:

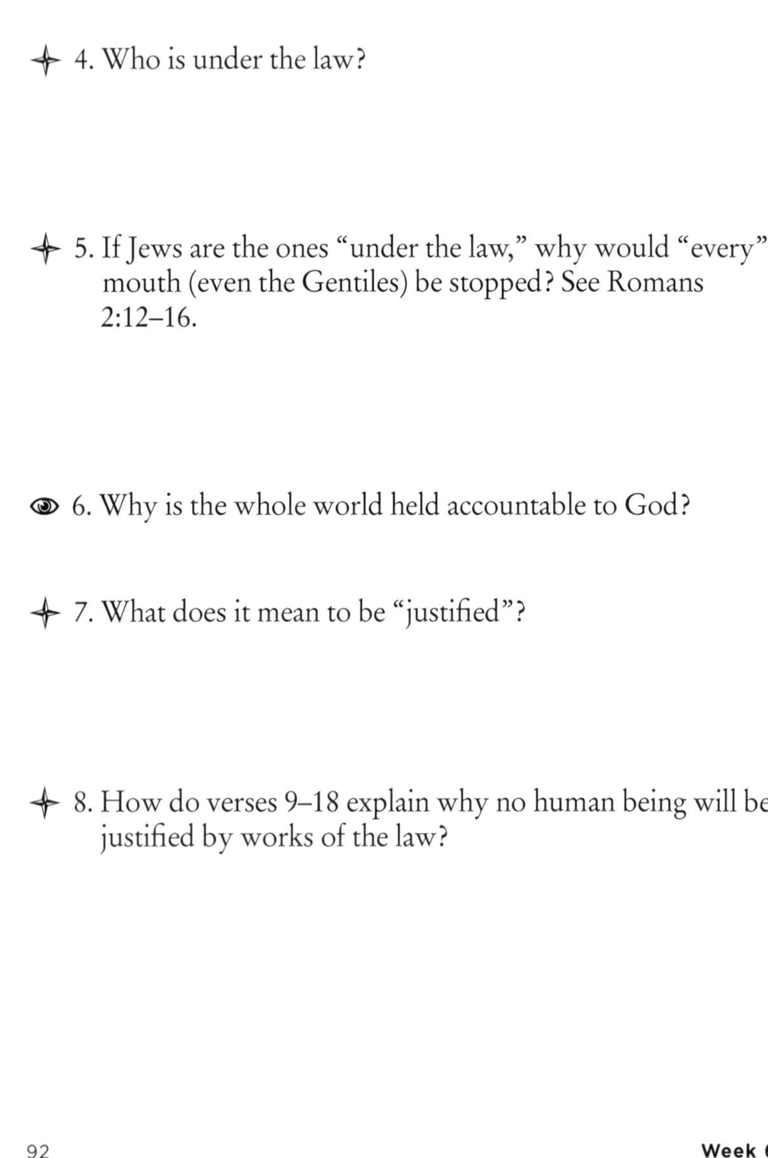

2. Now what do we know (verse 19)?

3. What are the effects of this?

4. Who is under the law?

5. If Jews are the ones "under the law," why would "every" mouth (even the Gentiles) be stopped? See Romans 2:12–16.

6. Why is the whole world held accountable to God?

7. What does it mean to be "justified"?

8. How do verses 9–18 explain why no human being will be justified by works of the law?

9. Are there ways that you try to be justified in God's sight by works of the law? Consider your family life, friendships, work, and church life.

10. How does Romans 1:17 address those areas of your life?

11. If you are a mother, are there ways you may be inadvertently teaching your children they can be justified by works of the law?

11. What comes through the law?

12. Explain how knowledge of sin comes through the law:

13. Are there times you've seen your sin through the law—reading your Bible or hearing it preached? What was your response to this?

Pray, then read Romans 1:18–3:20.

✦ 1. Romans 3:19–20 is the culmination of Paul's argument from 1:18–3:18. Explain why the whole world is held accountable to God:

✦ 2. Explain why no human being will be justified in the sight of God by works of the law:

♥ 3. If we cannot be justified by works of the law, why is the Bible so important? What does reading the Bible and hearing it read, sung, prayed, and preached in church do for us? (Remember 3:2 as well as 3:20.)

♥ 4. Next week, we'll study 3:21 and following. Read 3:21–24. After reading about the gravity of our sin and our accountability before God, what hope do these verses give you?

WEEK 7: ROMANS 3:21-27

This week praise God for putting forward his Son and pray to
see the glory of his righteousness more clearly.

DAY 1

Pray, then read Romans 3:9–30.

Romans 3:21–22

✦ 1. What does Romans 3:20 have to do with righteousness
and the law?

✦ 2. What does "But now" at the beginning of verse 21 signal?

👁 3. What has now been manifested and apart from what?

👁 4. What do the Law and the Prophets have to do with the
righteousness of God?

👁 5. Through what is the righteousness of God applied and to
whom is it available?

✦ 6. What does "righteousness of God" mean? (What does

"righteousness" mean and what does it mean that it is "of God"?)

✦ 7. How has it been "manifested"? (You might want to look up *manifested* in a dictionary.) See Romans 1:16–17.

✦ 8. What does it mean that this righteousness has "been manifested apart from the law"? (In what way did the law show God's righteousness and how is the manifestation of it now different?) See verse 20.

♥ 9. What does it mean for you in your life that the righteousness of God has been manifested apart from the law?

✦10. What does it mean that "the Law and the Prophets bear witness to it"? See Luke 24:25–27 and 44–47.

❤11. Can you think of some specific ways the Old Testament bears witness to Jesus?

✦12. What does the fact that the Old Testament bears witness to Jesus tell us about:

• God's character?

• God's plan?

• Jesus himself?

❤13. What is the importance of the Old Testament for Christians and how should we read it?

✦14. What does it mean to have "faith in Jesus Christ"?

15. Do you have faith in Jesus Christ? What do you believe about him?

Pray, then read Romans 3:9–31.

Romans 3:22b–24a

1. The first half of verse 22 tells us the righteousness of God is "for all who believe." How does Paul reinforce that statement in the second half of the verse?

2. Why would Paul make this statement? What distinction might the first century Roman church have made?

3. What are the two reasons there is no distinction?

4. What does it mean to sin?

5. What does it mean to fall short of God's glory? How are sinning and falling short of God's glory related? See Romans 1:21–22.

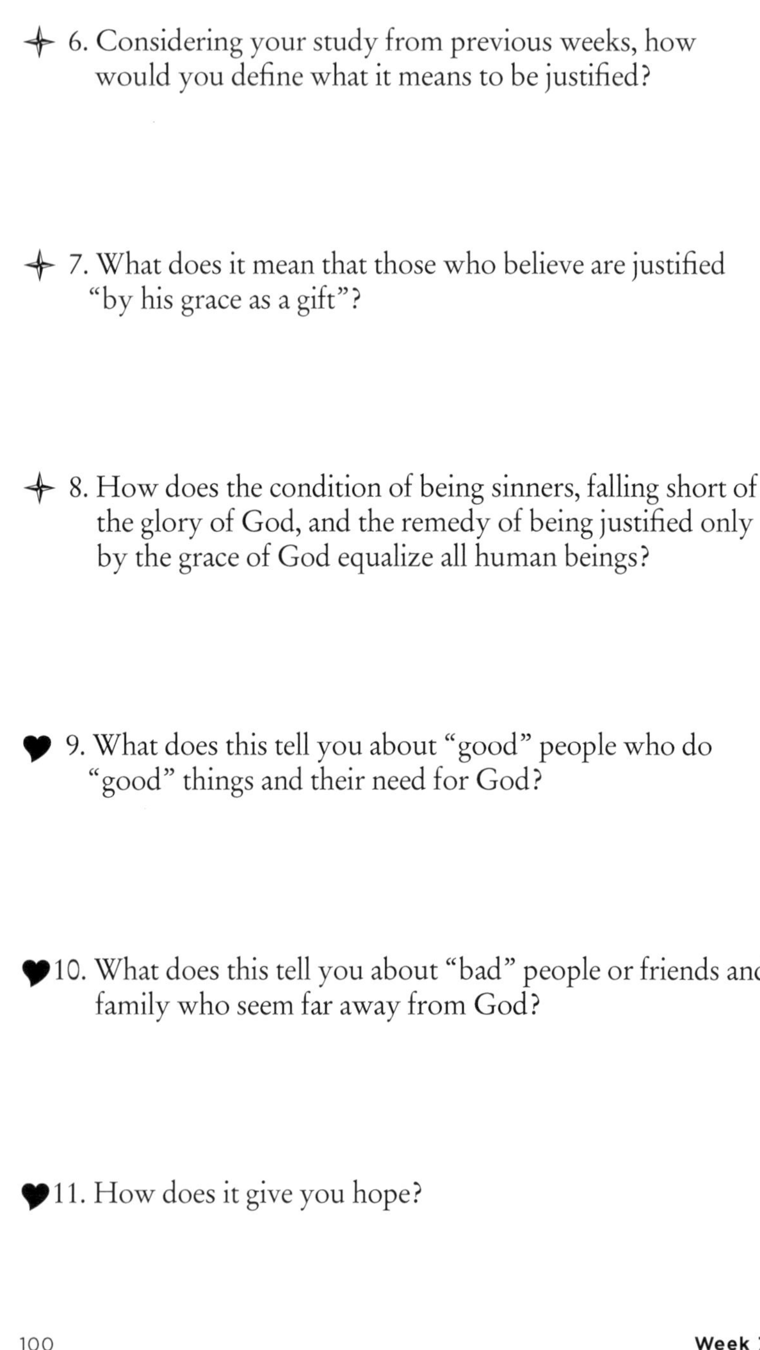

✦ 6. Considering your study from previous weeks, how would you define what it means to be justified?

✦ 7. What does it mean that those who believe are justified "by his grace as a gift"?

✦ 8. How does the condition of being sinners, falling short of the glory of God, and the remedy of being justified only by the grace of God equalize all human beings?

♥ 9. What does this tell you about "good" people who do "good" things and their need for God?

♥ 10. What does this tell you about "bad" people or friends and family who seem far away from God?

♥ 11. How does it give you hope?

Pray, then read Romans 3:20–30.

Romans 3:24b–25a

👁 1. How are people justified by God's grace? What is the gift?

👁 2. In whom is redemption?

✦ 3. What does "redemption" mean? See Exodus 20:2; Galatians 3:10–13; and Colossians 1:13–14.

✦ 4. Verse 24 describes this redemption as being "in Christ Jesus." See also Ephesians 1:7 and Colossians 1:14. What does this mean and what does it have to do with verse 22?

👁 5. How did God secure this redemption through Jesus?

✦ 6. God the Father put Jesus "forward as a propitiation." Was Jesus an innocent victim of God's wrath, or was he a willing sacrifice for sinners? See Hebrews 9:14 and 12:2.

👁 7. How is this redemption received?

✦ 8. What does "propitiation" mean and why is it necessary?
   See Romans 1:18. See also Colossians 3:5–6 and 1 John
   2:2.

✦ 9. What does it have to do with the blood of Jesus? See
   Romans 5:9; Ephesians 2:13; Colossians 1:20; and
   Hebrews 9:22.

✦10. What does it mean for this redemption to be "received by
   faith"?

♥11. How is biblical propitiation different from the pagan idea
   of offering up an innocent child to assuage the wrath of
   an angry God? See John 10:30, 14:9–11; Hebrews 1:3;
   Philippians 2:5–11 and Hebrews 12:2.

12. What is your reaction to Jesus's blood being shed to satisfy God's wrath against sinners? How is this personal to you?

Pray, then read Romans 3:20–30.

Romans 3:25b–26

1. What does "this" in verse 25b refer to?

2. What was "this" to show?

3. Why did God show his righteousness in this way at this time?

4. What does "forbearance" mean?

5. What does it mean that God "passed over former sins" and what does that have to do with "divine forbearance"? See Romans 2:4 and 2 Peter 3:9.

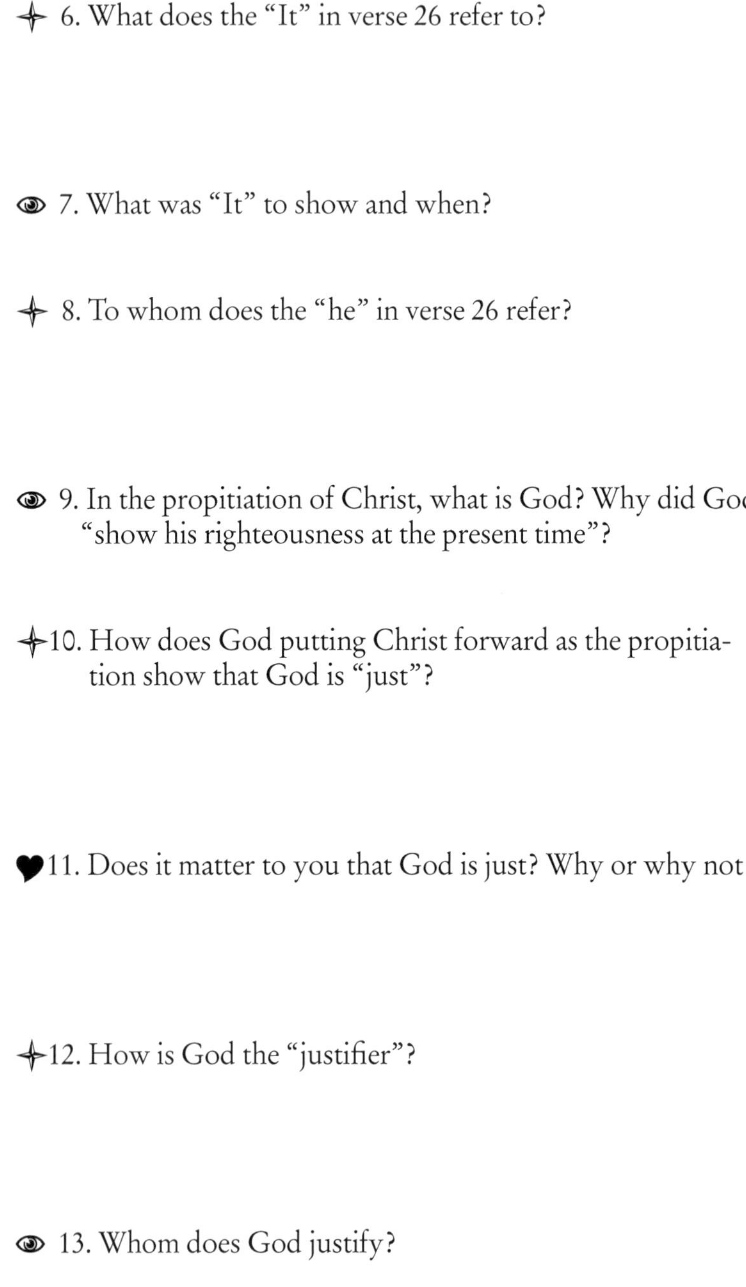

✦ 6. What does the "It" in verse 26 refer to?

👁 7. What was "It" to show and when?

✦ 8. To whom does the "he" in verse 26 refer?

👁 9. In the propitiation of Christ, what is God? Why did God "show his righteousness at the present time"?

✦10. How does God putting Christ forward as the propitiation show that God is "just"?

♥11. Does it matter to you that God is just? Why or why not?

✦12. How is God the "justifier"?

👁 13. Whom does God justify?

14. What does it tell you about God that he is both just and the justifier?

15. What does it tell you about Jesus that God justifies "the one who has faith in Jesus"?

16. How do these truths about God's character and the finished work of Christ motivate you to praise God?

17. How do these truths motivate you to share the gospel with others?

DAY 5

Pray, then read Romans 3.

Romans 3:21–27

1. God **revealing something** or **putting something on display** is a repeated theme in verses 21–26. List the words Paul uses to refer to such revelation/display, and then tell **what** is being revealed/displayed as well as **how** or **in what way**. (The first one is done for you.)

- Verse _21_ Word: _Manifested___________
  What is revealed/displayed?
    The righteousness of God

  How is it revealed?
    Apart from the law

- Verse ______ Word: __________________
  What is revealed/displayed?

  How is it revealed?

- Verse ______ Word: __________________
  What is revealed/displayed?

  How is it revealed?

- Verse ______ Word: __________________
  What is revealed/displayed?

  How is it revealed?

👁 2. How many times is God's righteousness mentioned in these verses?

Week 7

3. What fully reveals the righteousness of God, and what does this tell us?

4. In Islam "Allah" is said to be forgiving. There is no sacrifice for sinners, but Allah can decide to forgive some people's sins (and those who are more obedient are more likely to be forgiven). What does this say about whether the Muslim god is righteous and just?

5. If the true God is truly just, what is the problem every sinner faces (including me and you)?

6. Another repeated theme in these verses is faith. How many times is "faith" or "believe" repeated, and what does this tell us?

7. How would you describe the world's definition of "faith"?

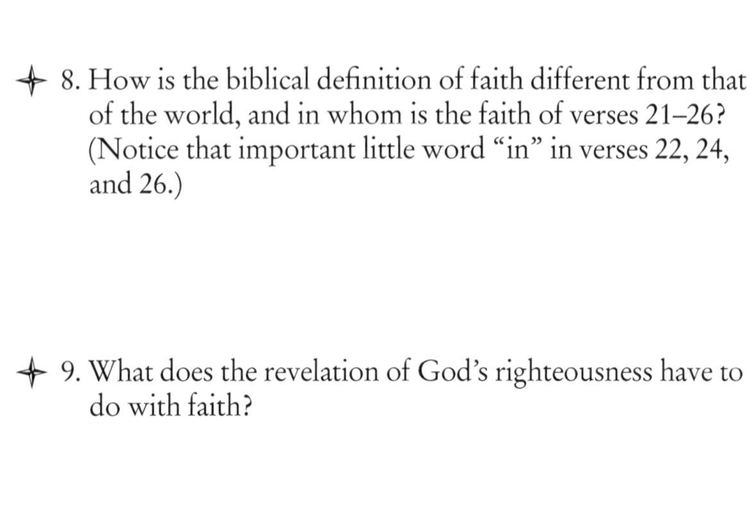

✦ 8. How is the biblical definition of faith different from that of the world, and in whom is the faith of verses 21–26? (Notice that important little word "in" in verses 22, 24, and 26.)

✦ 9. What does the revelation of God's righteousness have to do with faith?

✦10. How is a person credited with the righteousness of God?

◉11. What is the question Paul asks at the beginning of verse 27?

◉12. How does he answer the question?

✦13. Explain Paul's argument. How do verses 21–26 lead to boasting being excluded?

14. Why would Paul feel the need to make this argument?

15. How are we Christians tempted to boast in our salvation (especially those of us who have grown up in the church)?

16. What are some ways we can cultivate personal humility toward God and others, especially with regard to our salvation?

17. What are some ways that churches boast instead of giving God the glory?

18. What is the remedy for this?

19. Boasting is excluded, but what should be our response to our salvation that God has accomplished through Jesus's atoning (propitiating) death?

WEEK 8: ROMANS 3:27–4:12

Pray to have a firm grasp of justification by faith and to grow in living by faith.

DAY 1

Pray, then read Romans 3:19–4:8.

Romans 3:27–28

👁 1. What question does Paul ask, and how does he answer it?

👁 2. "By what kind of law" is boasting excluded?

👁 3. What kind of law would not exclude boasting?

👁 4. What kind of law does Paul say "we hold"?

✦ 5. What does Paul mean by "the law of faith"?

✦ 6. How is "the law of faith" different from "a law of works"?

✦ 7. To whom does "we" in verse 28 refer?

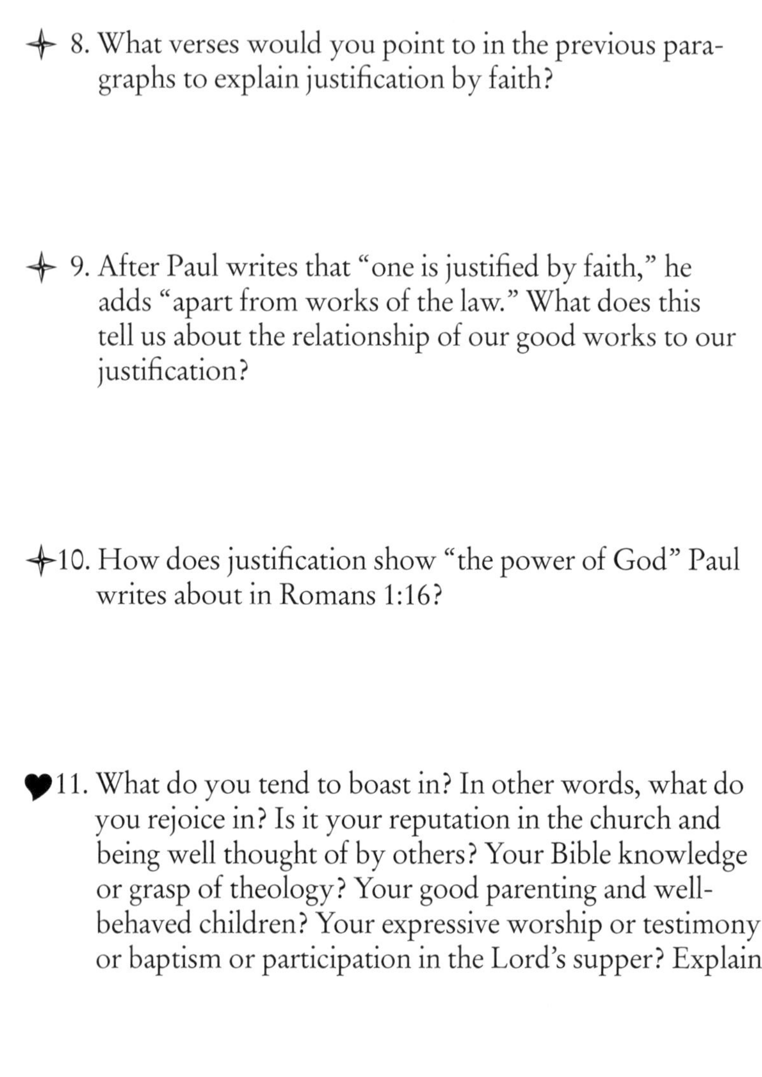

✦ 8. What verses would you point to in the previous paragraphs to explain justification by faith?

✦ 9. After Paul writes that "one is justified by faith," he adds "apart from works of the law." What does this tell us about the relationship of our good works to our justification?

✦10. How does justification show "the power of God" Paul writes about in Romans 1:16?

♥11. What do you tend to boast in? In other words, what do you rejoice in? Is it your reputation in the church and being well thought of by others? Your Bible knowledge or grasp of theology? Your good parenting and well-behaved children? Your expressive worship or testimony or baptism or participation in the Lord's supper? Explain:

♥12. How does "the law of faith" exclude boasting in these things?

Pray, then read Romans 3:19–31.

Romans 3:29–30

👁 1. What two questions does Paul ask in verse 29?

👁 2. How does he answer the questions?

👁 3. What is the basis for God being the God of both Jews and Gentiles?

✦ 4. What is Paul saying about God when he writes, "God is one"? What are the implications of God being the one God of all peoples?

👁 5. What will God do?

✦ 6. How does verse 28 relate to verses 29–30?

✦ 7. What do these verses tell us about the one way to be justi-fied (made right with God)?

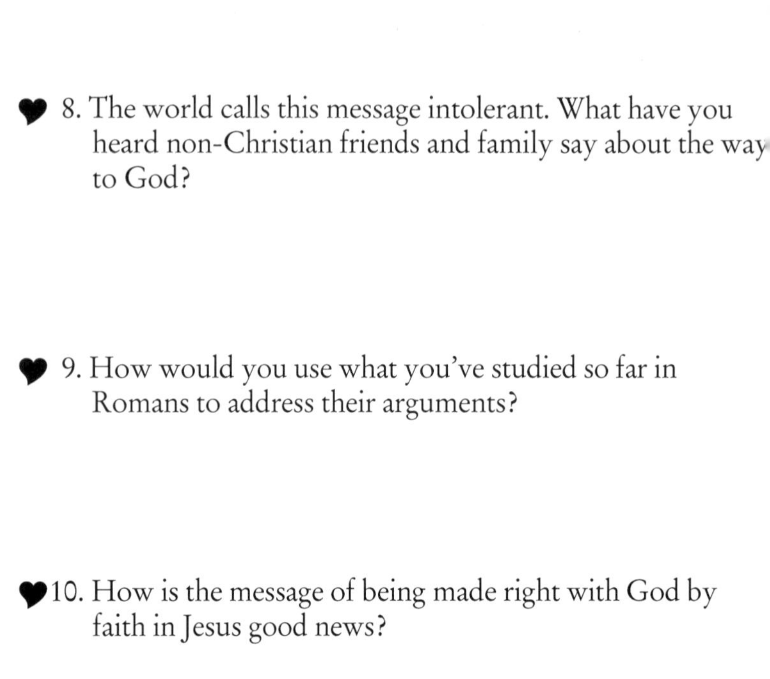

8. The world calls this message intolerant. What have you heard non-Christian friends and family say about the way to God?

9. How would you use what you've studied so far in Romans to address their arguments?

10. How is the message of being made right with God by faith in Jesus good news?

11. How does this message increase our joy and put to shame our boasting in other things?

DAY 3

Pray, then read Romans 3:8–4:5.

Romans 3:31–4:3

1. What question does Paul ask in 3:31?

✦ 2. Why does he ask this question here? (Notice the "then" in the question.)

◉ 3. How does he answer the question?

◉ 4. What do we do by faith?

✦ 5. What does it mean to "uphold the law" by faith? See Romans 6:4 and 8:4.

✦ 6. In Romans 3:20 Paul writes that no one will be justified by works of the law, but that "through the law comes knowledge of sin." What does this purpose of the law have to do with upholding the law by faith? How does the law help us to live by faith?

♥ 7. What does it look like in your life to "uphold the law" by faith?

👁 8. What question does Paul ask about Abraham, the forefather of the Jews?

👁 9. If Abraham was justified by works, what would he have?

👁10. Does he have something to boast about before God?

👁11. Why does he not have something to boast about? "[W]hat does the Scripture say?"

✦12. Romans 4:3 quotes from Genesis 15:6. Read Genesis 15:1–6 and describe the situation. What specifically does Abraham believe?

✦13. Why would Paul bring up Abraham here?

♥14. When you search your heart, what ways do you find that you try to boast before God? Do you boast in your upbringing or accomplishments? Your church activities or service to the community? Your parenting or good works? Your theological or Bible knowledge?

15. Explain why we should not boast about these things before God:

16. What should our attitude toward these good things be?

DAY 4

Pray, then read Romans 3:27 –4:12.

Romans 4:4–8

1. How are the wages of "one who works" counted?

2. Whose "faith is counted as righteousness"?

3. Who is "him" in verse 5? Who justifies the ungodly? (Romans 3:24–26)

4. What does David speak of?

👁 5. What is the righteousness apart from?

✦ 6. Who was David, and why would Paul bring him up here?

👁 7. What does David say about the blessing of righteousness apart from works?

✦ 8. Verses 7–8 quote from the first two verses of Psalm 32. Read Psalm 32 and answer the following questions:

A. Read verses 1–2 and 10–11, the top and the tail of Psalm 32. (If the top and tail of a passage is similar, it can signal the main point of the text.) What is the tone of these verses, and what is David's hope?

B. What happens in verses 3–5 of Psalm 32?

C. What is David's condition before he repents?

D. Continue reading verses 6–7. What is David's confidence after he repents?

E. How does David counsel others in verses 8–10?

F. ◉ Who does steadfast love surround?

G. In Psalm 32, David seems to firmly believe that God will forgive him and not count his sins against him. He even seems to believe that he and others are "righteous" and "upright in heart," yet he is a sinner who needs to repent. How can these two things both be true? (What line in Psalm 32:10 corresponds with Romans 4:5?)

✦ 9. David clearly believes his sins will be forgiven and he will be counted righteous before God, but in previous weeks we have read that one can only be justified through faith in Jesus Christ because he is the one who took the punishment for the sins of his people. David lived over a thousand years before Jesus was crucified. How could David be justified through faith? Read Hebrews 11:1–2, 13–16 and 39–40.

✦10. What does this have to do with Romans 3:25–26?

✦11. How is Jesus the ultimate fulfillment of Psalm 32?

♥12. Do you like the idea of your righteousness being apart from your works? Why or why not?

♥13. Would you rather have the wages you are due or have your faith counted as righteousness? Explain your answer:

14. David says "Blessed are those whose" sins are forgiven. He says to "Be glad," "rejoice," and "shout for joy"! What is your response to having your sins forgiven and being counted righteous before God?

15. David in Psalm 32:8–11 instructs and exhorts his people to repent of their sin and trust in the Lord. In light of the joy of having your sins forgiven and being counted righteous before God, do you desire to instruct and exhort others? What opportunities have you had to do this?

DAY 5

Pray, then read Romans 4.

Romans 4:9–12

1. What question does Paul ask in verse 9?

2. What "blessing" is he referring to?

3. What do Paul and those with him say?

◉ 4. Paul then asks how and when faith was counted to Abraham as righteousness. How does he begin to answer at the end of verse 10?

◉ 5. What did Abraham receive from God?

◉ 6. What did the sign of circumcision signify?

✦ 7. Read Genesis 17:1–14. What was circumcision? What were the circumstances of God's command for Abraham and his family to be circumcised? And what did it mean?

✦ 8. Why was circumcision so important to the Jews? What did it show?

✦ 9. What does it mean for circumcision to be "a seal of the righteousness that he had by faith"? How is God's covenant related to Abraham being counted righteous?

◉10. What was the purpose of the sign of circumcision being given to Abraham *after* God counted him righteous by faith? (What two groups does this make Abraham the father of?)

✦11. Why would Paul call Abraham the "father" of the uncircumcised who believe and the circumcised who walk in the footsteps of his faith? What's the significance of Abraham being the father of these two groups?

✦12. The account of Abraham's belief being "counted to him as righteousness" is found in Genesis 15. The account of Abraham's circumcision is in Genesis 17—this would have been decades after Genesis 15. Explain Paul's argument about the timing of Abraham's circumcision in your own words:

♥13. Some say the God of the Old Testament is a God of law, but the God of the New Testament is the God of grace. How would you use what you've studied this week to argue that he is the same God whose character never changes?

14. How does this bring you comfort and give you confidence?

15. How does understanding that righteousness comes by faith alone, not by works of the law, promote unity in a local church, particularly in a church with people from different family, ethnic, and cultural backgrounds?

16. How does this give you confidence to share the gospel with people from different backgrounds?

WEEK 9: ROMANS 4:13-24

Pray for a deeper understanding of the promise of God and what
it means to be counted righteous by faith.

**(Note: Day 4 of this week has a lot of reading about Abraham
from Genesis. You may want to split it into two days.)**

DAY 1

Pray, then read Romans 4.

Romans 4:13–25

◉ 1. The word "promise" (or "promised") is repeated 5 times
in these verses. List the verses where you find the word:

✧ 2. What does the repetition of this word tell you about this
passage of Scripture?

✧ 3. What is a "promise"?

◉ 4. Who made the promise?

◉ 5. To whom was the promise made?

◉ 6. What is the promise?

7. Read Genesis 17:1–8. What is the promise in Genesis 17, and how is the promise described differently by Paul in Romans 4?

8. Read the promise to Abraham in Genesis 12:1–3. After reading Genesis 12 and 17 explain how Paul can interpret the promise to Abraham and his offspring as inheriting the "world":

9. When you make a promise, what can prevent you from carrying out your promise?

10. Can anything thwart God from carrying out his promise? What about God's character makes his promises trustworthy? See Romans 3:4, 4:17b; Ephesians 1:11 and Psalm 139:16–18.

11. How do these characteristics affect whether you believe God's promises?

Pray, then read Romans 3:20–4:25.

Romans 4:13–15

👁 1. How did the promise to Abraham come? How did it not come?

👁 2. To whom is the promise also given, and what is the promise?

✦ 3. What is an "heir"?

✦ 4. Remind yourself of your answers to questions 6 and 7 from yesterday. Also read Genesis 1:26–28 and Revelation 21:1–5. What does "heir of the world" mean?

👁 5. Who is Abraham's offspring according to Galatians 3:16?

✦ 6. How are Abraham's offspring described in Romans 4:16 and 4:11b–12? And what does this have to do with Jesus?

7. What would result if "the adherents of the law" were to be heirs?

8. What does it mean for faith to be "null" and the promise "void"?

9. Why would this be the result?

10. Where is there no transgression?

11. When Paul writes there is no "transgression" where there is no law, what does he mean? (He cannot mean there is no sin because that would contradict what he's already written in chapters 1–3 about all sinning.) See also 3:20.

12. How does adherence to the law void the promise and nullify faith, and what does God's wrath have to do with it?

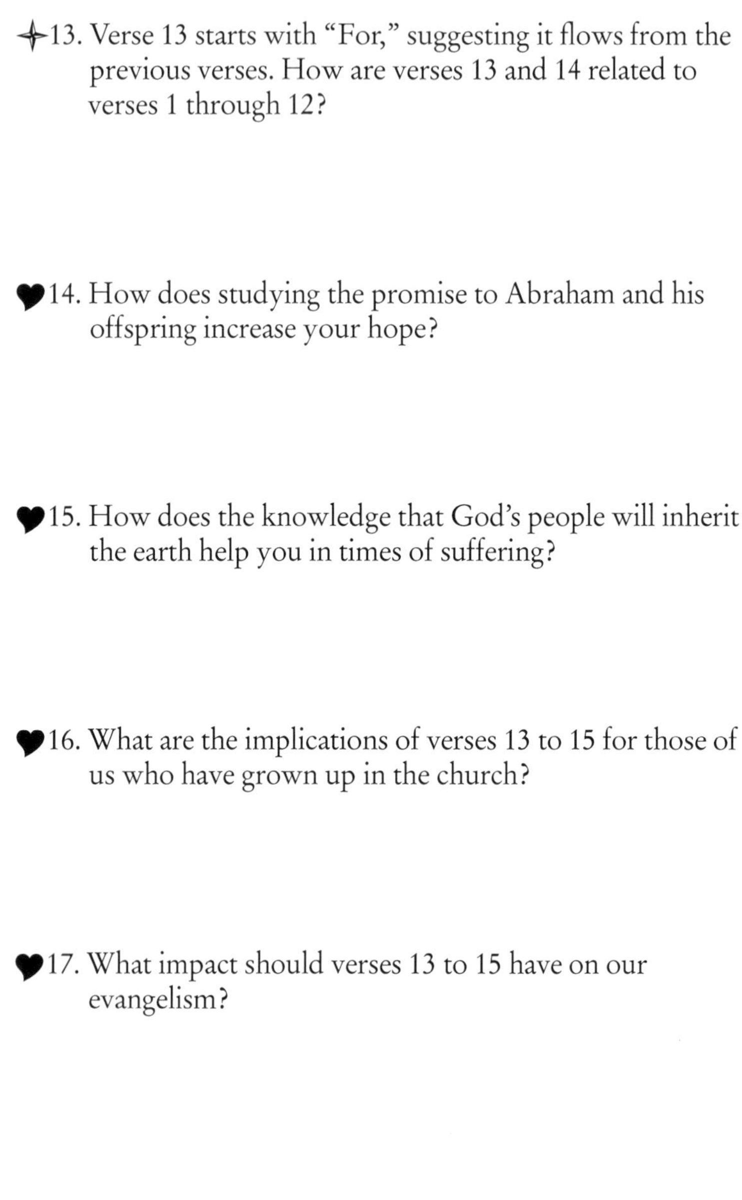

✦13. Verse 13 starts with "For," suggesting it flows from the previous verses. How are verses 13 and 14 related to verses 1 through 12?

♥14. How does studying the promise to Abraham and his offspring increase your hope?

♥15. How does the knowledge that God's people will inherit the earth help you in times of suffering?

♥16. What are the implications of verses 13 to 15 for those of us who have grown up in the church?

♥17. What impact should verses 13 to 15 have on our evangelism?

Pray, then read Romans 4:11–25.

Romans 4:16–17

👁 1. What does the promise depend on and why?

👁 2. How are Abraham's offspring described?

✦ 3. Who is Paul referring to when he writes, "the adherent of the law"?

✦ 4. What does it mean to share "the faith of Abraham"?

✦ 5. Does Paul mean for these two groups of people to be in contrast? In other words, is "the adherent of the law" guaranteed the promise even if he does not share "the faith of Abraham"? What word is repeated in the verse to help you determine your answer to this question?

✦ 6. What does it mean that the promise rests on grace, and what does that have to do with faith?

✦ 7. Sum up what it means to be Abraham's offspring (see also verse 12) and what it means for the promise to be "guaranteed" to Abraham's offspring? How is it guaranteed?

👁 8. How is Abraham described, and what is written about him?

👁 9. In whom did Abraham believe, and how is God described?

✦10. What specifically would Abraham have believed when God said, "I have made you the father of many nations"? See Genesis 17:1–5. How does this relate to the description of God at the end of 4:17?

✦11. What is Paul referring to when he writes that God "gives life to the dead"? See John 5:21 and Hebrews 11:17–19.

✦12. What is Paul referring to when he writes that God "calls into existence the things that do not exist"? See Ephesians 2:10 and Hebrews 11:3, 11–12.

♥13. What do these things tell us about God?

♥14. Before God called him out of his old life into relationship with him, Abraham was a pagan who worshipped idols, which means he depended on those idols to grant his desires. What people or things do you tend to depend on?

✦15. What does it mean to believe God's promise to Abraham this side of the cross? What do those who today share "the faith of Abraham" believe and what does it have to do with God giving life to the dead and calling into existence the things that do not exist?

♥16. Do you believe the promise to Abraham? How does believing this affect your day-to-day life?

Pray, then read Romans 4:13–25.

Romans 4:18–21

👁 1. What did Abraham "in hope [believe] against hope"?

👁 2. What had he been told?

👁 3. What did not cause him to weaken in his faith? How old was Abraham, and what was wrong with Sarah?

✦ 4. How does this explain why Paul describes Abraham as hoping against hope? What would have to happen for God to fulfill his promise to Abraham?

👁 5. What did not make Abraham waver concerning God's promise? Instead of wavering, what did Abraham do?

👁 6. To whom did Abraham give glory, and of what was he convinced?

✦ 7. What do verses 19–21 tell us about the nature of faith?

8. The account of Abraham is recorded in Genesis 12–25. Skim the following passages and jot down a sentence or two summarizing the accounts.

• Genesis 12:1–7:

• Genesis 12:10–20:

• Genesis 15:

• Genesis 16:

• Genesis 17:1–8:

• Genesis 17:15–23:

- Genesis 18:

- Genesis 20:

- Genesis 21:1–7:

- Genesis 22:1–18:

✦ 9. What are some ways God shows his faithfulness to Abraham in these passages?

✦10. How was Abraham's faith shown?

11. Abraham was certainly not perfect. How can Paul claim
    that "no unbelief made [Abraham] waver" in light of
    what happened in Genesis 12:10–20, Genesis 16 and 20?

12. Abraham waited a long time for God's promise to be
    fulfilled, and yet verse 20 tells us he grew in his faith dur-
    ing the waiting. How do you see this growth reflected in
    the account of Abraham in Genesis, and what enabled his
    growth?

13. Are you fully convinced that God is able to do what he
    has promised—that through Jesus we will be heirs of the
    world? What does this have to do with God giving "life
    to the dead and [calling] into existence the things that do
    not exist"? See Ephesians 2:1–7 and 1 Peter 2:9–10.

14. How does living according to this promise give glory to
    God?

♥ 15. What enables our growth in faith while we wait? How
are these things similar to what enabled Abraham to grow
in faith? What do we have that he didn't have?

DAY 5

Pray, then read Romans 4.

Romans 4:22–24

👁 1. What was the result of Abraham's unwavering faith that
God was able to do what he had promised?

✦ 2. Verse 22 is the conclusion of a sustained argument by
Paul in chapter 4. Go back through chapter 4 and find
all the references to "count" or "counted." (If you take
notes in your Bible, you may wish to circle them.) What
is Paul's argument about Abraham? Why is Abraham's
faith "counted to him as righteousness"?

👁 3. For whose sake were the words, "it was counted to him"
written? And to whom will it be counted?

✦ 4. What does it tell you about Abraham (and about other
Old Testament saints) that this was written not only for

                                                    Week 9

him but for us also? What does it tell you about the Old
Testament itself?

✦ 5. What does it tell you about the plan of God?

✦ 6. Why does Paul bring up God raising Jesus from the dead
here? How does that connect with previous verses?

✦ 7. Why do you think Paul makes this painstaking argument
about Abraham and then applies it to those "who believe
in him who raised from the dead Jesus our Lord"?

✦ 8. Explain in your own words who is counted righteous
before God:

♥ 9. Do you "believe in him who raised from the dead Jesus our Lord"? If so, what is your response to being counted righteous?

♥10. A theological term for being counted righteous is "imputed righteousness." It means to attribute or credit to a person righteousness that is derived from another. This is a doctrine in which to delight! What are some ways we can remind each other from day to day of imputed righteousness?

✦11. We are counted righteous by faith apart from works but true faith has certain characteristics. Look back at verses 17–24 and think about Abraham's life. What are some characteristics of faith that is counted righteous?

♥12. How are these traits characteristic of your faith?

WEEK 10: ROMANS 4:25 AND ROMANS 1–4 REVIEW

This week rejoice that Jesus "was delivered up for our trespasses and raised for our justification," and ask the Father to show you the glory of what he has done through Christ.

DAY 1

Pray, then read through Romans 1–4.

1. Romans 4:25 tells of the fulfillment of God's promise to Abraham and his children. Write out 4:25 but replace "who" with "Jesus our Lord":

2. What is Paul referring to when he writes that Jesus "was delivered up"?

3. What does "trespasses" mean?

4. Explain for whom and why Jesus was crucified:

5. What is Paul referring to when he writes that Jesus was "raised"?

✦ 6. What does "justification" mean?

✦ 7. What did the resurrection prove? See Romans 1:4.

♥ 8. Romans 6:5–11 describes the believer being united with the Lord Jesus in his death and resurrection. If Jesus's resurrection shows that the Father accepted his sacrifice, looking on him with favor, and that sin and death were conquered, what does our being raised with Jesus (Ephesians 2:6) tell us about the Father's disposition toward us?

♥ 9. How does knowing God approves of you affect your relationship with him?

♥ 10. How does God's approval of you affect the way you handle flattery or encouragement from others?

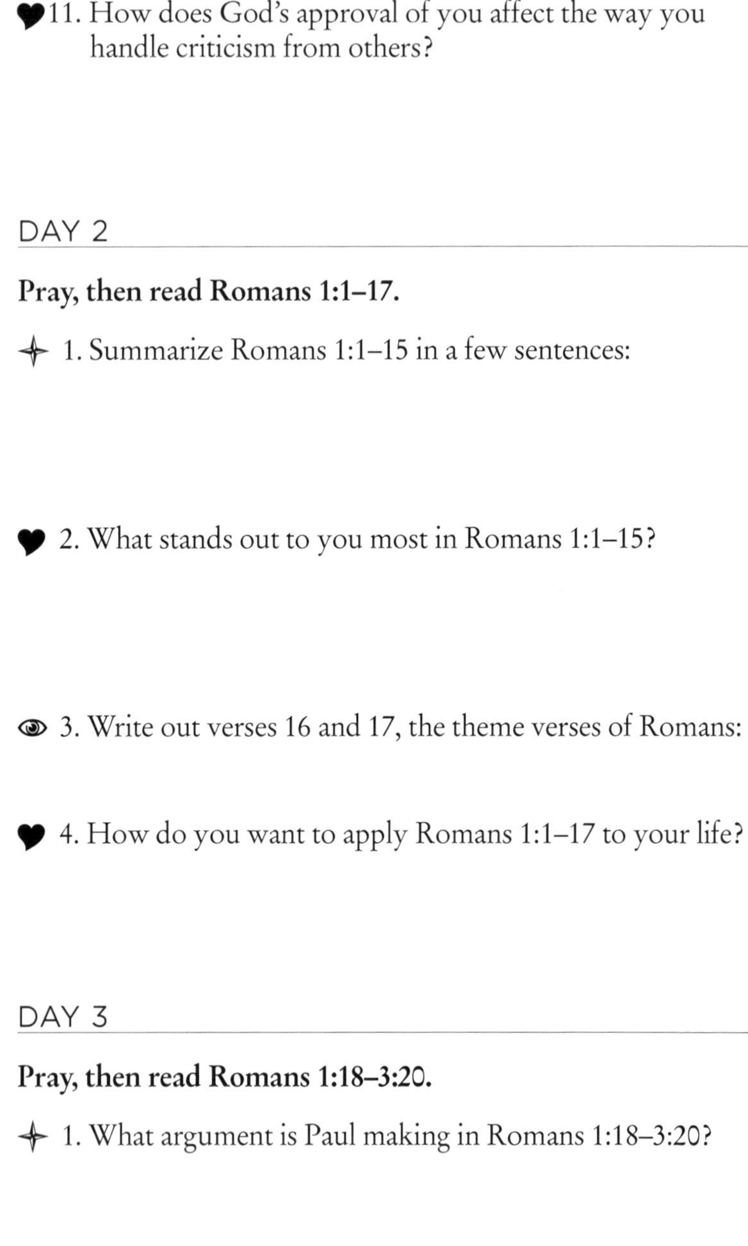

11. How does God's approval of you affect the way you handle criticism from others?

DAY 2

Pray, then read Romans 1:1–17.

1. Summarize Romans 1:1–15 in a few sentences:

2. What stands out to you most in Romans 1:1–15?

3. Write out verses 16 and 17, the theme verses of Romans:

4. How do you want to apply Romans 1:1–17 to your life?

DAY 3

Pray, then read Romans 1:18–3:20.

1. What argument is Paul making in Romans 1:18–3:20?

✦ 2. Why is it so important for Paul to make this argument?

✦ 3. Paul repeatedly mentions Jews and Gentiles in these
   verses and puts them on equal footing. Why is the apostle
   emphasizing this at the beginning of his letter?

✦ 4. What do you learn about God from these chapters of
   Romans?

♥ 5. How will you apply the truths of Romans 1:18–3:20 to
   your life?

DAY 4

Pray, then read Romans 3:21–4:25.

✦ 1. Summarize Paul's argument in Romans 3:21–4:25:

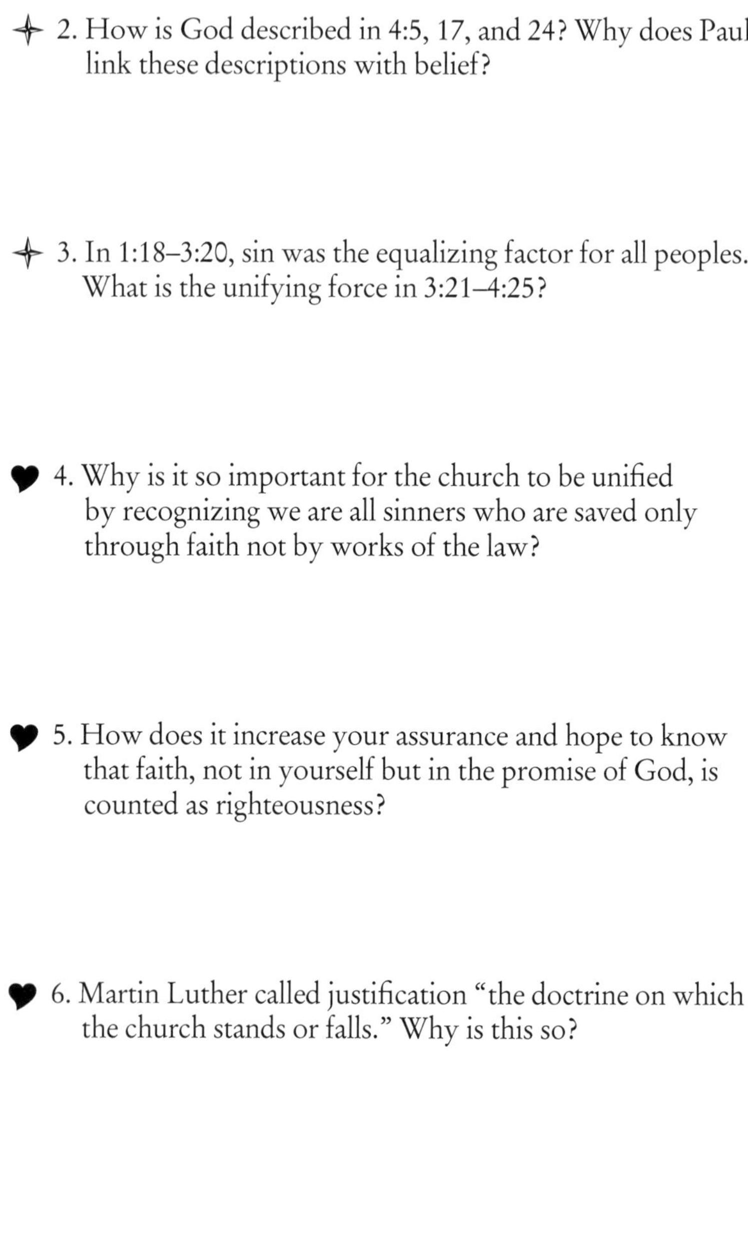

2. How is God described in 4:5, 17, and 24? Why does Paul link these descriptions with belief?

3. In 1:18–3:20, sin was the equalizing factor for all peoples. What is the unifying force in 3:21–4:25?

4. Why is it so important for the church to be unified by recognizing we are all sinners who are saved only through faith not by works of the law?

5. How does it increase your assurance and hope to know that faith, not in yourself but in the promise of God, is counted as righteousness?

6. Martin Luther called justification "the doctrine on which the church stands or falls." Why is this so?

✦ 7. Thinking about the purpose of this letter as stated at the beginning and end of Romans (1:5b and 16:25–26), why is it important for Paul to stress unity?

♥ 8. How will you apply Romans 3:21–4:25 to your life?

DAY 5

Pray, then read Romans 4:23–5:1.

✦ 1. How does Romans 4:23–25 relate to Romans 1:16–17?

◉ 2. What does Romans 5:1 say we have, and how?

◉ 3. Through whom do we have peace with God?

✦ 4. How does 5:1 follow from 4:24–25?

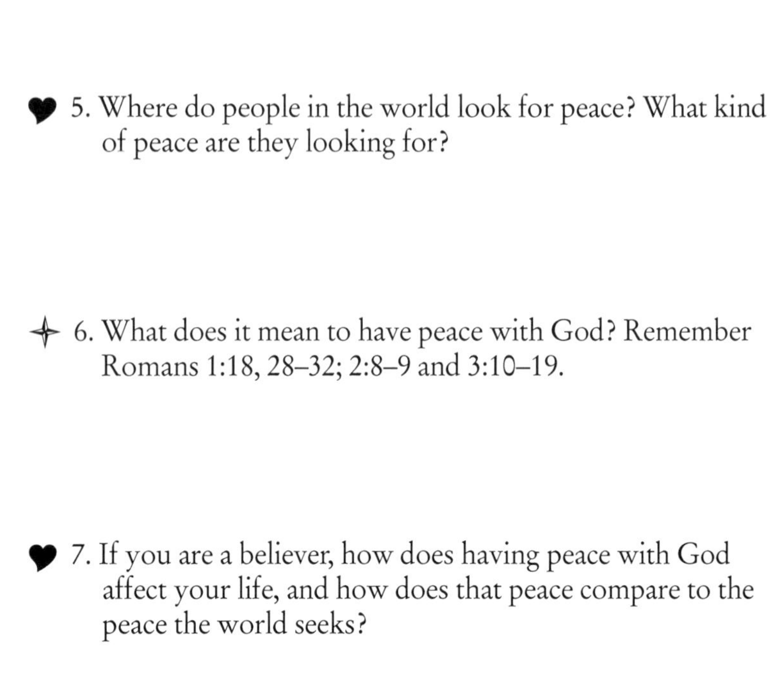

5. Where do people in the world look for peace? What kind of peace are they looking for?

6. What does it mean to have peace with God? Remember Romans 1:18, 28–32; 2:8–9 and 3:10–19.

7. If you are a believer, how does having peace with God affect your life, and how does that peace compare to the peace the world seeks?

8. Write a short summary of Romans 1–4, tracing Paul's argument, and end by writing out 5:1:

9. How has studying Romans 1–4 affected your life?

WEEK 11: ROMANS 5:1–11

This week, praise God for sending Christ to die for the ungodly, and pray this knowledge would increase your joy even amid suffering.

DAY 1

Pray, then read Romans 4:13–5:5.

Romans 5:1–2a

✦ 1. Notice the "therefore" that begins chapter 5. Everything that follows the therefore is based on the previous four chapters. Verse 25 is the climax of chapters 1–4. Summarize what it means that Jesus "was delivered up for our trespasses and raised for our justification":

◉ 2. How is justification applied to us personally?

◉ 3. What do we have as a result of this justification, and through whom are we justified?

✦ 4. Is this peace an objective fact or a subjective feeling? Explain your answer, remembering the first four chapters of Romans:

5. How could you use 4:24–5:1 to share the gospel with a friend who struggles with anxiety?

6. How are faith and our Lord Jesus Christ connected to result in justification?

7. What have we also obtained by faith, and what is our posture in it?

8. What does it mean for us to have access "into this grace in which we stand"?

9. Adam and Eve sinned and were banished from God's presence in the Garden of Eden. Later, God dwelt in the midst of his people Israel but behind a curtain in the Holy of Holies in the tabernacle and temple. Only the high priest could enter into God's immediate presence behind the curtain, and that only once a year with a blood sacrifice. See Leviticus 16 and Hebrews 9:6–7 and compare Matthew 27:51. What does it mean for you personally to have peace with God and stand before him in grace?

❤10. How does this affect your worship?

❤11. How does God's presence with you affect how you read your Bible and pray?

DAY 2

Pray, then read Romans 4:23–5:11.

Romans 5:2b–4

👁 1. In what do we rejoice, and through whom do we rejoice?

✦ 2. What is biblical hope and how is it related to faith? See 5:5; Hebrews 11:1; and 1 Peter 1:3–5.

✦ 3. What does the glory of God refer to, and what does it mean for the Christian to have the hope of the glory of God? See Romans 8:16–18, 23–24, 29–30; John 17:1–5, 10; and Hebrews 1:3.

4. What about this hope causes Christians to rejoice?

5. How do you see your past, present and future coming together in verses 1–2?

6. What else do Christians rejoice in?

7. What types of things would suffering involve?

8. What knowledge results in rejoicing? Write out the chain of production from suffering to hope using arrows:

9. What does "endurance" mean?

10. What does "character" mean?

✦11. How does suffering produce endurance and endurance produce character? See James 1:2–4 and 1 Peter 1:6–7.

✦12. How does the character that results from suffering produce hope?

✦13. Why would this character and hope result in rejoicing?

♥14. In what ways have you seen this chain from suffering to hope work in your life? Has your suffering resulted in rejoicing?

♥15. Some of us have suffered in excruciating ways for which we will never know the purpose in this life. Looking carefully at these verses, what is the key to our suffering ultimately resulting not in despair but in rejoicing?

16. Take some time to pray for a brother or sister in Christ who is going through or has gone through inexplicable suffering. Pray that he or she would know there is purpose in the suffering. Pray that his or her suffering would result in treasuring Christ more and increased hope.

DAY 3

Pray, then read Romans 5:1–11.

Romans 5:5

1. What is true about the hope that is produced by the chain of suffering, endurance, and character?

2. Why does this hope not put us to shame?

3. What is Paul referring to when he writes about God's love being "poured into our hearts through the Holy Spirit"? See John 3:3–8 and Titus 3:4–7.

4. What does "poured" suggest about God's love for us?

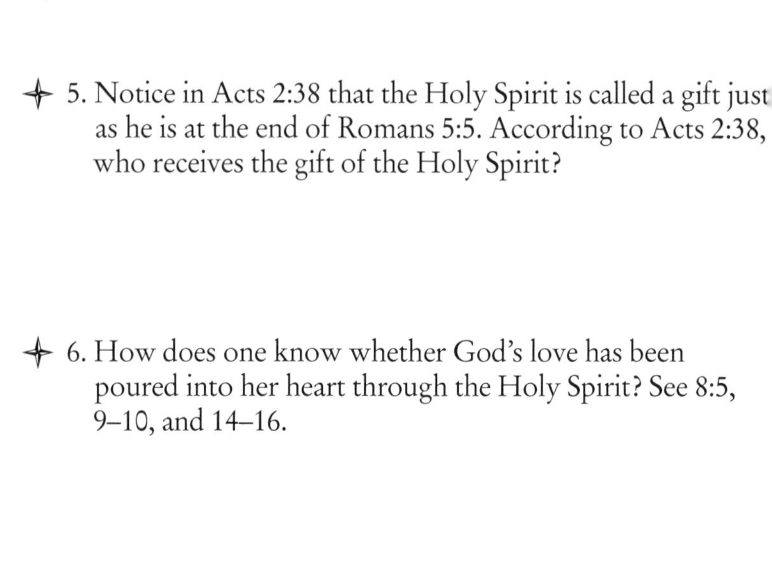

✦ 5. Notice in Acts 2:38 that the Holy Spirit is called a gift just as he is at the end of Romans 5:5. According to Acts 2:38, who receives the gift of the Holy Spirit?

✦ 6. How does one know whether God's love has been poured into her heart through the Holy Spirit? See 8:5, 9–10, and 14–16.

♥ 7. How does God's love being poured into our hearts give us confidence in our hope?

✦ 8. How is the chain of suffering that leads to hope related to peace with and access to God?

♥ 9. How does confidence in God's love for us lead us to hold on all the more tightly to hope in future glory when we are going through suffering?

10. How would you use these verses to address those who call themselves Christians and claim that Christians don't suffer sickness or financial difficulty if they have enough faith?

Pray, then read Romans 4:23–5:11.

Romans 5:6–8

1. What did Christ do "while we were still weak"?

2. What does Paul mean by "weak"? The Greek word could also be translated "powerless." Notice the other words in verses 6–10 that correspond with "weak" in verse 6.

3. In what sense did Christ die "at the right time"? How does this phrase highlight our weakness?

4. What does this tell us about God?

5. Who might one die for?

6. What circumstances can you think of in which someone might die for a righteous or good person?

7. One might die for a person who is righteous or good, but how does God show his love for us?

8. Why do you think Paul contrasts dying for a good person with what God has done for us in Christ? What does this highlight about God?

9. What does it tell us about us?

10. What does it tell us about Christ?

11. What is your response to this kind of love for you?

12. Verse 6 begins with "For." How are verses 6 and following connected to the previous verses?

13. How does knowing the depth of God's love for you —as seen in Christ's dying for you while you were his enemy—increase your hope?

14. How does it increase your hope for friends and family and others you are sharing the gospel with who have not yet received God's love?

15. What does this display of love teach you about loving others who are difficult to love?

DAY 5

Pray, then read Romans 4:23–5:15.

Romans 5:9–11

1. By what have we been justified?

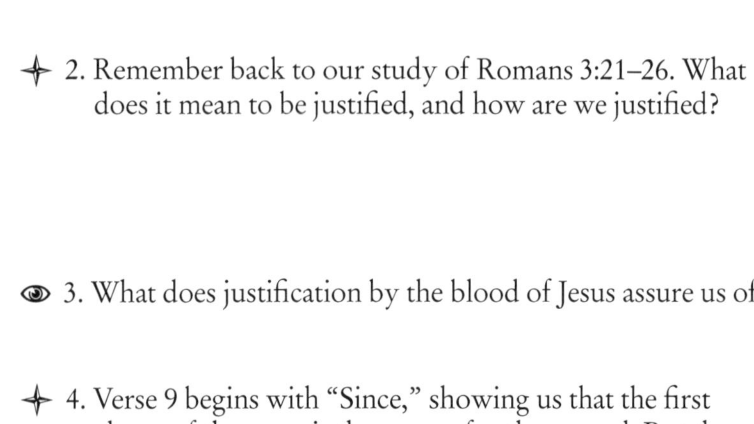

✦ 2. Remember back to our study of Romans 3:21–26. What does it mean to be justified, and how are we justified?

◉ 3. What does justification by the blood of Jesus assure us of?

✦ 4. Verse 9 begins with "Since," showing us that the first clause of the verse is the reason for the second. But the word "therefore" is also inserted after "Since." What is "therefore" pointing back to in the previous verses, and what does this have to do with being saved from the wrath of God?

◉ 5. What happened while we were God's enemies, and how did it happen?

◉ 6. If this happened, what is "much more" certain?

✦ 7. What does Christ's life refer to? Read Romans 4:24–25.

✦ 8. How would you summarize Paul's argument in verses
6–10?

✦ 9. When we speak of "salvation" or "getting saved," we
often are referring to a one–time event, but Paul separates
out reconciliation and salvation here. What is the difference between reconciliation and salvation, and why does
Paul attribute reconciliation to Christ's death and salvation to Christ's life? See 2 Corinthians 4:10–14.

👁10. In Romans 5:11, what does Paul add to reconciliation and
salvation?

👁11. What does he repeat about our Lord Jesus Christ?

✦12. Why do you think Paul repeats that we have been reconciled three times in the closing verses of this section?

❤13. Do you have confidence that you have been saved from
the wrath of God and will be saved by the life of Christ?
If so, what does that confidence look like?

♥14. Do you "rejoice in God through our Lord Jesus Christ" because you have been reconciled to the Father through the Son? What does that rejoicing look like?

✦15. How does reconciliation relate to the chain of suffering to hope in verses 3–5?

WEEK 12: ROMANS 5:12–21

Pray this week to be found in Christ and his righteousness, and
for the Holy Spirit to work that righteousness out in your life by
God's grace.

DAY 1

Pray, then read Romans 5:6–21.

Romans 5:12–14

👁 1. How did sin come into the world, and how did death
come into the world?

👁 2. What did death do, and why?

👁 3. When was sin in the world but not counted, and why?

👁 4. Yet what did death do from Adam to Moses, and over
whom did death do it?

👁 5. Who was Adam? Why is he significant in the biblical
account?

✦ 6. According to Genesis 2:15–17 and 3:1–7, how did sin
come into the world through the one man Adam?

✦ 7. According to Genesis 2:15–17 and 3:16–19 and 23–24,
      what was the punishment for Adam's sin?

✦ 8. Adam did not die an immediate physical death, but he did
      eventually physically die. How does Ephesians 2:1–3 fur-
      ther explain the kind of death Adam immediately faced?

✦ 9. To what law is Paul referring in Romans 5:13, and how
      do you know?

✦10. God did not give the law until Moses, who lived long
      after Adam's fall. Paul says in verses 13–14 that "sin is
      not counted where there is no law. Yet death reigned
      from Adam to Moses," so clearly people were punished
      for their sin. How was the people-of-that-time's sinning
      different than the transgression of Adam? What does this
      tell us about directly disobeying the word of God?

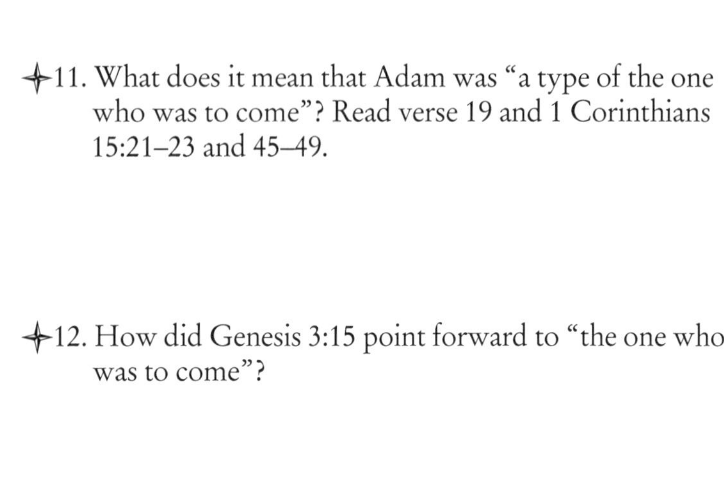

✦11. What does it mean that Adam was "a type of the one who was to come"? Read verse 19 and 1 Corinthians 15:21–23 and 45–49.

✦12. How did Genesis 3:15 point forward to "the one who was to come"?

♥13. Verses 12–14 and following give us the doctrine of original sin. What do these verses tell you about yourself apart from Christ?

♥14. What do they tell you about God?

♥15. Some claim that Adam is a fictional character Israel used to explain the existence of sin. Based on Paul's argument in Romans 5:12–21, did Paul believe Adam was a historical person? Explain your answer using the text. Why is this important? See also Paul's comments in Acts 17:26 and 1 Corinthians 15:44b–47.

Pray, then read Romans 5:10–21.

Romans 5:15–17

1. Why does Paul begin verse 15 with a "But"? What contrast is he highlighting?

2. What is not like the trespass?

3. What is the free gift? Remember Romans 3:23–25 and 4:4–5 and see 5:17.

4. Why is the free gift not like the trespass?

5. Write in your own words how the grace of God and the free gift by the grace of Jesus Christ compare with the one man's trespass. What is Paul emphasizing in verse 15?

7. What is the free gift also not like?

👁 8. Why is the free gift not like the result of the one man's sin?

✦ 9. To what do the many trespasses refer?

✦10. How does the free gift contrast with the result of Adam's sin? (Write verse 16 in your own words.)

✦11. Why do you think Paul here contrasts the free gift with the trespass instead of with the law?

👁12. Through whom did death reign and why?

👁13. If death reigned through one man, who will reign in life through the one man Jesus Christ?

✦14. What does it mean to reign in life? How does God's commission to the first man help us to know what it means

to reign in life? Read Genesis 1:26–28 and Revelation
2:26–27, 3:21 and 22:5.

✦15. Verses 15–17 set up two categories of human beings:
those who are in Adam and those who are in Christ.
How does the reign of death in Adam compare to the
reign of those who are "in Christ" Also see 1 Corinthians
15:21–22?

♥16. Which of these categories are you in, and what are the
implications for your life according to Romans 5:15–17?

DAY 3

Pray, then read Romans 5:12–21.

Romans 5:18–19

👁 1. What did the one trespass lead to?

👁 2. What did one act of righteousness lead to?

👁 3. What did the one man's disobedience make many?

👁 4. What will the one man's obedience make many to be?

✦ 5. Do you see how verses 18 and 19 are parallel? How does the one trespass correspond to the one man's disobedience, and to what do these refer?

✦ 6. How does the one act of righteousness (v. 18) correspond to the one man's obedience (v. 19), and to what do these refer?

✦ 7. Verse 19 begins with "For." It gives the explanation for verse 18. Why does being made sinners result in condemnation? How did the one man's disobedience lead to condemnation for all men?

✦ 8. How does being made righteous result in justification and life? How does the one man's obedience lead to justification and life for all men?

✦ 9. The "all men" in verse 18 corresponds to "the many" in verse 19. Who are the "all men" and "the many" who

   Week 12

were made sinners and are condemned? And who are the "all men" and "the many" who will be made righteous and are justified and live?

💚 10. Some would use the "all men" of verse 18 to argue universalism—the view that all people will finally be saved. How would you address this argument using verses 1 and 17 of chapter 5? See also 3:26–28 and 4:23–25. And why do you think Paul uses the term "all men"?

✦ 11. Summarize Paul's argument from verses 18–19:

💚 12. How can verses 18–19 be a comfort to you when you are discouraged by sin in your life?

DAY 4

Pray, then read Romans 5:18–6:4.

Romans 5:20–21

👁 1. What did the law do?

◉ 2. What happened where sin increased?

✦ 3. What does Paul mean when he writes that the law came "to increase the trespass"? How did the law increase the trespass?

✦ 4. How is it that grace abounded more where sin increased?

◉ 5. What is the purpose for grace abounding where sin has increased?

◉ 6. Through what does grace reign, and what does this lead to?

✦ 7. Paul bookends this passage, verses 12–21, with the law. Why do you think Paul brings up the law in verses 13 and 20? How does grace compare to the law?

✦ 8. What does it mean for grace to "reign through righteous-ness"? Through whose righteousness does it reign?

✦ 9. How does that righteousness lead "to eternal life through Jesus Christ our Lord"? See Romans 4:22–25.

✦10. Write verses 20–21 in your own words and explain why this sentence is a fitting conclusion to this section of Romans.

♥11. What do you learn about Jesus from these verses?

♥12. What does it mean for your life that grace reigns?

Pray, then read Romans 5:10–6:4.

Romans 5:12–21

👁 1. Reread Romans 5:12–21 and write down any repeated words and phrases:

👁 2. Write down any contrasts you see:

✦ 3. As you see the contrasts and repeated words and phrases, what stands out to you?

✦ 4. Considering the contrasts and repeated words and phrases and remembering your study from the previous days, how would you summarize Paul's argument in this section? (You may want to go back and read your answers to Day 1, Question 9; Day 2, Questions 5, 10, and 15; Day 3, Question 11; and Day 4, Question 10.)

💜 5. Romans 5:12–21 compares humanity in Adam to new humanity in Christ. What does it tell us about the nature of humanity in Adam? And how does that nature show itself even in little babies?

6. What does this section tell us about new humanity in Christ? And how does the new nature show itself in your life if you are in Christ?

7. Verse 12 begins with a "therefore." How are verses 12–21 connected with the peace with God, access by faith, and hope in suffering we read about at the beginning of chapter 5 and the reconciliation we see in the middle of the chapter? In other words, how is union with Christ related to the first half of the chapter?

8. Words like "abundant," "abound," and "much more" are used to describe the free gift of grace in Jesus Christ. If your identity is "in Christ" as opposed to Adam, what are the effects of overflowing grace in your life?

♥ 9. We see in verses 17 and 21 that righteousness and reigning are inseparably tied together. What does this mean for the Christian?

WEEK 13: ROMANS 6:1–14

Choose a particular sin that you struggle with and pray each day for the Lord to use what you learn in your study of Romans 6 to battle that sin.

DAY 1

Pray, then read Romans 5:18–6:14.

Romans 6:1–3

1. In the previous chapter, Paul emphasized the abundance of God's grace in Jesus Christ. What question does he ask about that grace?

2. Why does he ask this specific question? What argument is he anticipating?

3. What is Paul's clear answer to this question?

4. What question does he ask in response?

5. Rephrase this question into a declarative statement:

6. What were all who were baptized into Christ Jesus also baptized into?

✦ 7. Paul assumes that all the early Roman Christians were baptized. How does the physical act of being baptized present a picture of us dying with Christ?

✦ 8. What does it mean to "live in" sin?

✦ 9. Can one who has died to sin still live in it? What is Paul's point?

❤ 10. Have you died to sin, or are you still living in it? Explain your answer:

❤ 11. If you have been baptized into Christ, you have died to sin. In what ways do you struggle to believe this?

DAY 2

Pray, then read Romans 5:18–6:14.

Romans 6:4

👁 1. According to verse 4, what happened in baptism?

👁 2. What was the purpose of being baptized into Christ's death?

✦ 3. How does the physical act of baptism present a picture of us dying with Christ and being raised with him to new life?

✦ 4. Why would being baptized into Christ's death mean that **we** have died to sin? How is this related to 5:12–21?

✦ 5. What does it mean to "walk in newness of life" and how is Christ being raised from the dead related to our walking in this newness of life? See John 11:25; Ephesians 1:19–20, 2:10.

👁 6. How was Christ raised from the dead?

7. What does it mean that Christ was raised "by the glory
   of the Father"? And how does that phrase apply to our
   newness of life? See 2 Corinthians 13:4. See also John
   11:38–44.

8. How do verses 1–4 serve as a warning to women who call
   themselves Christian but are comfortably continuing in
   sin?

9. What particular sin are you praying about this week?
   How does knowing that in Christ's death you have died
   to sin and now, by the glory of the Father, have been
   raised to walk in newness of life affect how you deal with
   sin in your life?

10. How does knowing that the glory of the Father empow-
    ers you to "walk in newness of life" give you hope in the
    midst of your battle with sin?

DAY 3

Pray, then read Romans 5:20–6:14.

Romans 6:5–7

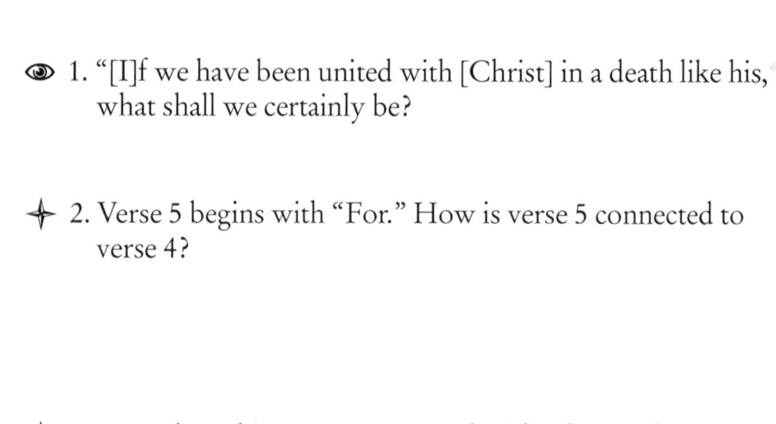

1. "[I]f we have been united with [Christ] in a death like his," what shall we certainly be?

2. Verse 5 begins with "For." How is verse 5 connected to verse 4?

3. How does this verse correspond with what Paul says about Adam and Christ in 5:12–21?

4. Verse 5 uses "have been" when referring to our union with Christ in his death, but it uses "shall…be" when referring to being united with Christ in his resurrection. Why is one "past tense" (it is actually the perfect tense, indicating that our union with Christ is ongoing) and the other future tense? What future event is Paul talking about?

5. If you are united to Christ, how does the certainty of verse 5 give you hope for the future?

👁 6. What do we know?

✦ 7. Jesus told his followers "If anyone would come after me, let him deny himself and take up his cross and follow me" (Mark 8:34). The cross was not just an instrument of suffering; it was an instrument of death. When Paul says, "our old self was crucified with [Christ]," what does he mean?

👁 8. Why did our old self have to be crucified with Christ?

👁 9. Why are we no longer enslaved to sin?

✦10. "Our old self" corresponds with "the body of sin." What does it mean for that body to "be brought to nothing"? (The Christian Standard Bible translates this phrase as "rendered powerless.") And how does this relate to "no longer [being] enslaved to sin"?

✦11. Paul writes in Galatians 2:20, "I have been crucified with Christ. It is no longer I who live, but Christ who lives in

me. And the life I now live in the flesh I live by faith in
the Son of God, who loved me and gave himself for me."
How does this verse add to your understanding of what
results from being crucified with Christ?

♥ 12. How does it help you in your fight against sin to remember that through being crucified with Christ sin has been
rendered powerless (brought to nothing!) in your life?

DAY 4

Pray, then read Romans 6:1–14.

Romans 6:8–11

👁 1. If we have died with Christ, what is also true?

👁 2. What do we know?

👁 3. Why is it that "death no longer has dominion over
[Christ]"? What do we know about Christ's death and
his life from verse 10?

✦ 4. What does it mean that we will "live with" Christ? Is this
true the moment we put our trust in him, or is it a prom-

ise for the future? Is there a sense in which we experience this already and a sense in which we don't fully experience it yet? What would you point to in verses 4–10 to make your argument?

5. Jesus lived a perfect, sinless life. In what sense did he die to sin, and what is the significance of that death being "once for all"? See Romans 3:25; 2 Corinthians 5:21; and Hebrews 9:11–14.

6. What does it mean that the life Jesus lives "he lives to God"?

7. In light of Jesus's life, what must we consider ourselves?

8. Taking into account verses 5–11, what does it mean to consider oneself dead to sin?

✦ 9. What does it mean to be "alive to God in Christ Jesus," and how does this phrase correspond to "[walking] in newness of life"?

♥10. What can help you continue to consider yourself "dead to sin and alive to God in Christ Jesus"?

♥11. Romans 6:1–11 describes what it is to be "in Christ" (no longer "in Adam"). If you are in Christ, you are "dead to sin and alive to God." How can this knowledge help you in your daily fight against sin? (Think particularly about the sin you're praying about this week.)

♥12. How do you see this actually taking place in your life?

♥13. Take some time to pray that being dead to sin and alive to God would be a reality that you experience in your daily life.

Pray, then read Romans 6.

Romans 6:12–14

1. Notice the "therefore" in verse 12. If we are "dead to sin and alive to God in Christ Jesus," what must we do about sin?

2. What does sin try to do?

3. Read Romans 1:28–32. The people of Romans 1 (those in Adam) have "debased mind[s]." They are "filled with" and "full of" sin. They are characterized by their sin. Why do you think Paul writes about sin here in Romans 6:12 as an entity to fight rather than a characterization of the believer? What's the difference between the believer and the unbeliever?

4. What does Paul mean by sin having passions, and how does sin work to reign in us, making us obey its passions?

5. Think about the sin you've been praying about this week. How does it try to make you obey its passions?

❺ 6. What are we to avoid doing so that sin will not reign?

❺ 7. What two things are we to do?

❺ 8. How are we described in verse 13?

✦ 9. How does this description correspond with the previous verses in chapter 6?

✦10. What does it mean to present our members to sin as instruments for unrighteousness? What does it mean to present our members to God as instruments for righteousness? What are these "members"?

✦11. The term "instruments" could also be translated "weapons." What picture is Paul drawing for us in these verses?

♥12. Considering the sin you are praying about, how have you presented your members to it as an instrument for unrighteousness in the past?; and, in the future, how can you present your members to God as instruments for righteousness?

13. Notice Paul does not write, "Do not present yourself to sin." The one who is truly in Christ belongs to him and cannot present herself to sin. What does it mean for you to *present yourself to God* as one who has been brought from death to life? How does this help you fight sin, using your members as weapons for righteousness?

14. What can we be confident of in our battle against sin?

15. Why can't sin have dominion over us?

16. Notice the certainty of verse 14. It does not begin with a conditional clause. It begins with a "For" not an "If." We should fight against sin because it will have no domin-ion over us. The battle must be fought but the victory is already won. Look back at 5:17, 20–21. How do these verses correspond with 6:14?

17. When you consider your battle with sin, what hope does this give you?

WEEK 14: ROMANS 6:15–7:6

If you are a Christian, praise God this week that you have been set free from sin and have become a slave to righteousness, receiving the free gift of God, "eternal life in Christ Jesus our Lord"!

DAY 1

Pray, then read Romans 6.

Romans 6:15–19

1. Paul asks, "What then?", connecting his next question to the previous verse. What question does he then ask?

2. Why might Christians' status as "not under law but under grace" cause them to think they are free to sin?

3. What is Paul's answer to his question?

4. Paul explains his answer further with another question. If one gives herself to anyone as an obedient slave, she is a slave to the one she obeys. What are the two choices, and where does each lead?

5. What does Paul thank God for?

✦ 6. What is the standard of teaching to which the members
of the church in Rome were committed? See Acts 2:42; 2
Timothy 1:13; and Titus 1:9; 2:1.

♥ 7. How does your life show that you are committed to this
standard?

♥ 8. How do churches today show their commitment to this
standard?

✦ 9. These people in the church at Rome were once slaves
to sin but now have been "set free from sin" and "have
become slaves of righteousness." Does this mean they no
longer sin? Explain your answer. What does it mean to be
a "slave of righteousness"?

✦10. What is the significance of being "obedient from the
heart"? See Romans 2:28–29.

◉11. How is Paul speaking, and why ?

◉12. They once presented their members as slaves to impurity and lawlessness. What did this lead to, and how does Paul now want them to use their members?

◉13. Where does slavery to righteousness lead?

✦14. Why do you think Paul needs to explain to his readers that he's speaking in human terms because of their natural limitations?

✦15. How does sin lead to more lawlessness, and how does righteousness lead to sanctification? (What does sanctification mean?)

♥16. Notice the progression when we present our members. If we present them as slaves to impurity and lawlessness, it leads to more lawlessness. If we present them as slaves to righteousness, it leads to sanctification. Have you seen this to be true? Give a real-life example of sin leading to more lawlessness and an example of righteousness leading to sanctification:

♥ 17. Think about the sin you are fighting. Do you find this principle of progression true when you give in to it? Do you find that your sanctification progresses when you refuse to give in to it and instead present your members as slaves to righteousness? Explain:

♥ 18. Considering this sin, what helps you be "obedient from the heart to the standard of teaching to which you were committed"?

DAY 2

Pray, then read Romans 6:1–7:6.

Romans 6:20–23

👁 1. When Paul's readers were slaves of sin, how were they free?

2. What does it mean to be "free in regard to righteousness"?

3. What does Paul ask his readers about fruit?

4. What things are they now ashamed of?

5. What would some of the fruit of those things have been? (See Romans 1:18–2:11)

6. What is the end of those things?

7. But now, what has happened?

8. To what does the fruit of slavery to God lead, and what is its end?

9. What kind of fruit comes from being a slave of God?

+10. What does "sanctification" mean and how does it come from the fruit of being slaves to God?

⊙11. How does Paul sum up this section and, indeed, the whole of chapter 6?

+12. Why would Paul use "wages" here, and how does that word contrast with "free gift" in the second clause of the verse?

+13. Think back through Romans 1–6. Why is 6:23 a fitting verse to reach a climax here in Romans?

+14. The "free gift of God is eternal life **in** Christ Jesus our Lord." How has Paul shown what it means to be "in Christ Jesus" in previous verses of chapter 6?

15. Have you been united to Christ in his death and resurrection? If so, explain. If not, write out questions you have about union with Christ.

16. If you are a Christian, think back on your non-Christian days. What fruit did your sin produce that you are now ashamed of? If you had stayed in that condition, how would that rotten fruit have grown? What would have been the result? If you are not a Christian, what fruit do you see your sin producing?

17. If you are now "in Christ Jesus," what fruit do you see in your life? How have your desires changed? What goodness is in your life that wouldn't be there if you were still in unbelief? (Take a moment to give thanks for God's work in your life.)

♥18. Considering the sin you've been praying about, the
    wages of that sin is death; but, praise God, his free gift is
    eternal life in Christ Jesus! We have seen that the super-
    abundance of that free gift of grace is much more than all
    of our sin. Any fight against sin is founded upon union
    with Christ and thereby being set free by his grace, but
    Paul also gives commands for fighting this fight. Go back
    through chapter 6 and find the imperatives (commands)
    Paul gives for fighting sin and walking "in newness of
    life." Underline or write out the imperatives and then
    explain how you can apply them directly to the sin.

♥19. Do you remember the questions Paul posed at the begin-
    ning (vss. 1–2) and middle (vs. 15) of chapter 6? What is
    the danger of separating the imperatives (commands) of
    the Christian life from the indicatives (statements of fact)
    of Christ's accomplishments?

♥20. How can you hold together both the indicative truths of
    the gospel and the imperative commands that flow from
    the gospel?

As we move on through our study of Romans, don't leave the indicatives or the imperatives behind — keep fighting that sin in light of Christ already conquering it!

DAY 3

Pray, then read Romans 6:20–7:6.

Romans 7:1–4

👁 1. What question does Paul ask?

👁 2. To whom is Paul speaking?

✦ 3. What law do the brothers (and sisters) know? To what law is Paul referring?

✦ 4. The Roman church had some Jewish believers but was mainly made up of Gentiles from a pagan background. What does Paul saying that they know the law suggest about what Gentiles would study and learn after being converted to Christianity?

♥ 5. What does this suggest to us about the value of knowing the whole of the Scriptures?

◉ 6. How long is the law binding on a person?

✦ 7. Paraphrase the example in verses 2–3 of a person no longer being bound to a law:

◉ 8. What is likewise true of the brothers?

◉ 9. How have they died to the law, and what is the result of
this death?

✦10. What does it mean to die to the law "through the body of
Christ"? To what is Paul referring?

✦11. Paul uses the example of how the death of a husband
releases the wife from being bound by the law of marriage. The wife does not die. Is Paul using an appropriate
analogy here? What in the phrase, "so that you may
belong to another," makes Paul's analogy fit? Why must
we die to the law to belong to Christ?

✦12. Paul begins chapter 7 with an "Or" that connects verse 1 and following to the previous verses. But verse 1 doesn't seem to follow directly from verses 20–23. What question is Paul continuing to answer, and what argument is he furthering? See 6:14.

✦13. To whom do the brothers and sisters now belong?

👁14. How is he described toward the end of verse 4?

✦15. Why do you think Paul reminds his readers here that Jesus "has been raised from the dead"?

❤16. Do you ever feel weighed down by rules in the Christian life? What would Paul say to you? Should guilt or fear motivate us or something else?

❤17. Belonging to Christ is a sweet truth of the Christian life. If you are a Christian, how does belonging to Christ make a difference in your life?

Pray, then read Romans 6:23–7:6.

Romans 7:4–5

👁 1. At the end of verse 4, what does Paul tell us is the purpose of dying to the law and belonging to Christ?

✦ 2. What does it mean to "bear fruit for God"? See also 6:22.

✦ 3. Why does dying to the law and belonging to Christ result in us bearing fruit for God? Why does it not simply result in us justifying our sin because we are no longer bound by the law?

❤ 4. If you belong to Christ, what fruit for God do you see being produced in your life?

👁 5. What was happening "while we were living in the flesh"?

✦ 6. What does Paul mean by "living in the flesh"?

✦ 7. In 7:7 and following, Paul will give a thorough explanation of what it means for sinful passions to be aroused
by the law. What is the purpose of the law according to
Romans 3:20?

✦ 8. What does it mean to "bear fruit for death"? How does
7:5 correspond to 6:21?

✦ 9. As we can see, Paul is continuing his argument from
chapter 6. Why is it so important for Paul to bring these
truths home to his readers? What does this have to do
with his missionary purpose (Romans 15:5–6, 20–28) for
writing the letter?

♥ 10. How does being under grace and belonging to another
(instead of being under the law) remove the law's power
to arouse the sinful passions in our hearts?

♥ 11. How can you use this truth to fight sinful passions that
battle in your heart?

Pray, then read Romans 7:1–12.

Romans 7:6

⊙ 1. What has happened now?

⊙ 2. How have Paul and his readers been released from the law?

✦ 3. In what way were they held captive by the law? See Galatians 3:23–24 and Hebrews 10:1–4, 11.

✦ 4. How did they die to the law? See Romans 7:4.

⊙ 5. What is the result of dying to the law and no longer being its captive?

✦ 6. Who is the Spirit, and what does it mean to "serve in the new way of the Spirit"? See Romans 1:4–5; 5:5; and 6:17.

✦ 7. How is belonging to Christ (v. 4) connected to God's love being "poured into our hearts through the Holy

Spirit who has been given to us" (5:5)? And what does this show us about the motivation for the "new way" of serving?

✦ 8. Upon whom must we rely to serve in this way?

✦ 9. What does serving "in the old way of the written code" mean? What motivates the person who serves in this way? What fruit does this bear?

♥ 10. Can one serve in both the old way of the law and the new way of the Spirit? What happens to the Christian who tries to do this?

♥ 11. How would you describe your motivation to serve or, as verse 4 puts it, "bear fruit for God"?

♥ 12. What are some practical ways to rely on the Spirit and increase our motivation to serve?

Pray this week to better understand your struggle with sin and to have confidence in that struggle that Jesus has paid for all your sin.

DAY 1

Pray, then read Romans 7:4–12.

Romans 7:7

👁 1. What question about the law does Paul ask?

✦ 2. Why is this a logical question to ask following what Paul writes in verses 4–6?

👁 3. What is Paul's forceful answer to the question?

👁 4. What does Paul say his condition would have been if it had not been for the law?

👁 5. What example does Paul use? What does he say he would not have known?

✦ 6. What does it mean to "covet"? See Exodus 20:17; Luke 12:15 and Ephesians 5:5.

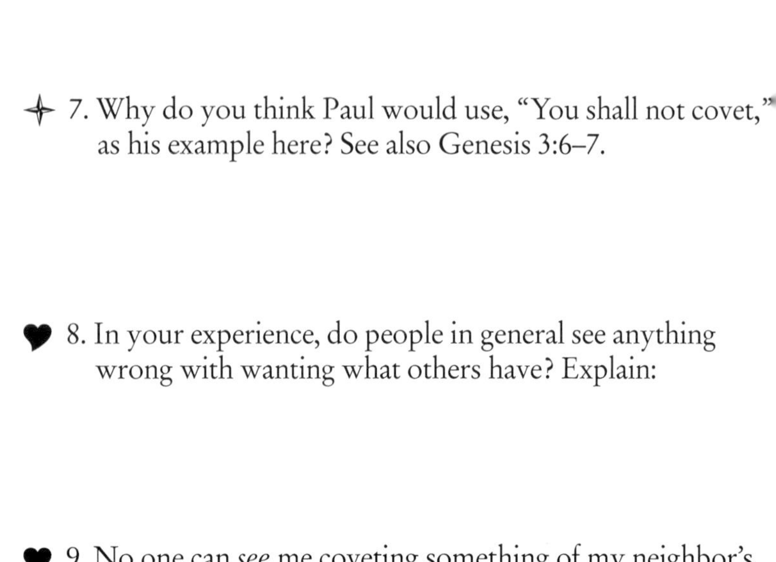

✦ 7. Why do you think Paul would use, "You shall not covet," as his example here? See also Genesis 3:6–7.

♥ 8. In your experience, do people in general see anything wrong with wanting what others have? Explain:

♥ 9. No one can *see* me coveting something of my neighbor's. It doesn't infringe on anyone else's rights. It is hidden in my heart. Why, then, is it a sin, and how does it bear fruit for death (7:5)?

✦10. What is the relationship of the law to sin? See also Romans 3:20.

✦11. Notice the past tense of the verbs in Romans 7:7. Who does the "I" represent in this verse, and what state of knowledge was he in without the law?

♥ 12. Can you think of a specific time the law has shown you
your sin? Explain:

♥ 13. What should our response be when God's word shows us
our sin?

Pray, then read Romans 7:7–20.

Romans 7:8–12

👁 1. What did sin seize, and what did it produce?

👁 2. What is the state of sin apart from the law?

✛ 3. What does Paul mean when he says that "apart from the
law, sin lies dead," but sin used the law to produce in him
"all kinds of covetousness"? Was Paul's sin non-existent
before he learned the law, or did the law stimulate his
covetousness?

👁 4. Paul "was once alive apart from the law." What happened
when the commandment came?

✦ 5. When Paul says he "was once alive apart from the law," he doesn't mean that he was living an abundant life headed for eternity. He means that his conscience wasn't bothering him. He led a free and easy life not recognizing his sin. How did the commandment bring Paul's sin to life, and what does he mean when he says he "died"? What is the difference in Paul before and after learning the commandments?

◉ 6. What had the commandment promised, but what did it prove to be?

✦ 7. How is it that the commandment promised life?

✦ 8. How did the commandment prove to be death instead?

◉ 9. Yesterday, we saw that the law shows us our sin. The law was the actor. In verses 8–11, sin becomes the actor. Paul repeats that *sin* seized an opportunity through the commandment (the law). From verse 11, list the two things sin used this opportunity to do:

✦10. What parallels do you see between Paul's experience with
the law and sin, and Adam's experience in the garden? See
Genesis 2:15–17 and 3:1–7.

✦11. If you are familiar with the Old Testament, what parallels
do you see between Paul and Israel's experience?

✦12. If Paul is writing this about himself, why do you think he
also alludes to the experience of Adam and Israel? What
is he trying to tell his readers?

♥13. What parallels do you see in your own experience with
the law and sin?

✦14. If, as we see in 1 Corinthians 15:56, "the power of sin
is the law," how do we relate to sin if we die to the law?
Remember Romans 7:4–6. What does this tell us about
the importance of being united to Christ in his death?

👁15. What conclusion does Paul make about the law in verse 12?

✦16. How does this conclusion follow from verses 7–11?

♥17. Why is it important for you that the law is not sin but is holy and righteous and good? How does this impact your life? See also Psalm 119:137–144.

DAY 3

Pray, then read Romans 7:7–25.

Romans 7:13–14

👁 1. What question does Paul ask, and how does he answer the question?

✦ 2. From the context, what is "that which is good"?

👁 3. What did bring death to Paul, and how?

4. What did sin producing death through the law ("that which is good") result in?

5. How does sin producing death through the law show sin to be sin, and what does that have to do with the law being good?

6. Explain how sin through the commandment might "become sinful beyond measure":

7. How does verse 13 correspond to the previous verses (7–12), and how are sin, the law, the increase of sin and death related? What argument is Paul making here?

8. Why is sin the culprit and not the law?

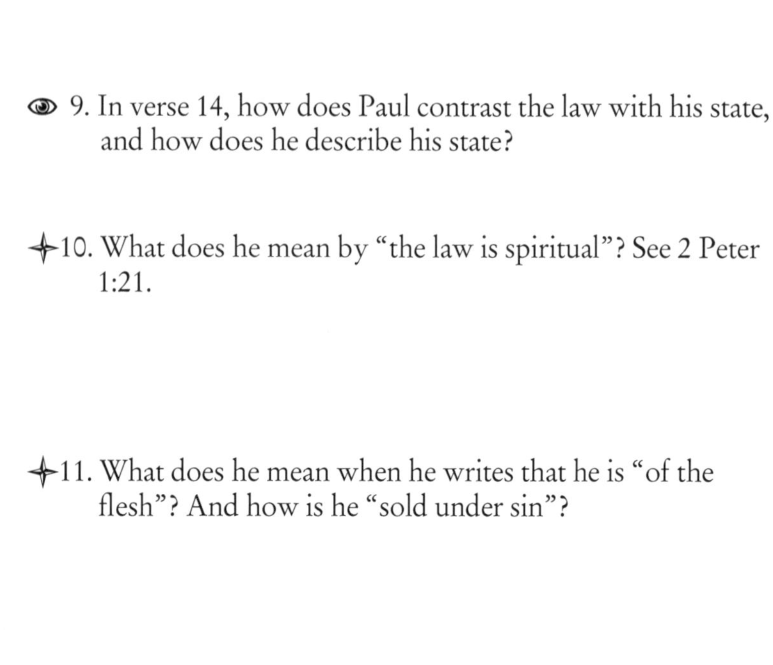

9. In verse 14, how does Paul contrast the law with his state, and how does he describe his state?

10. What does he mean by "the law is spiritual"? See 2 Peter 1:21.

11. What does he mean when he writes that he is "of the flesh"? And how is he "sold under sin"?

12. What does this tell us about what or who can be trusted for how to live this life? Will following our logic or emotions keep us on track or do we need something else?

13. If the law is holy and righteous and good but sin produces death through it and becomes sinful beyond measure, how should we relate to the law?

Pray, then read Romans 7.

Romans 7:15–20

👁 1. What does Paul not understand and why?

✦ 2. What does he mean by this? What does he want to do? What does he hate? How are his actions in conflict with his desires?

👁 3. What does Paul agree with when he does what he does not want?

✦ 4. How does doing what he does not want show agreement that the law is good, and what do his conflicting desires and actions have to do with him being "of the flesh" (v. 14)?

👁 5. What is true now for Paul, according to verse 17?

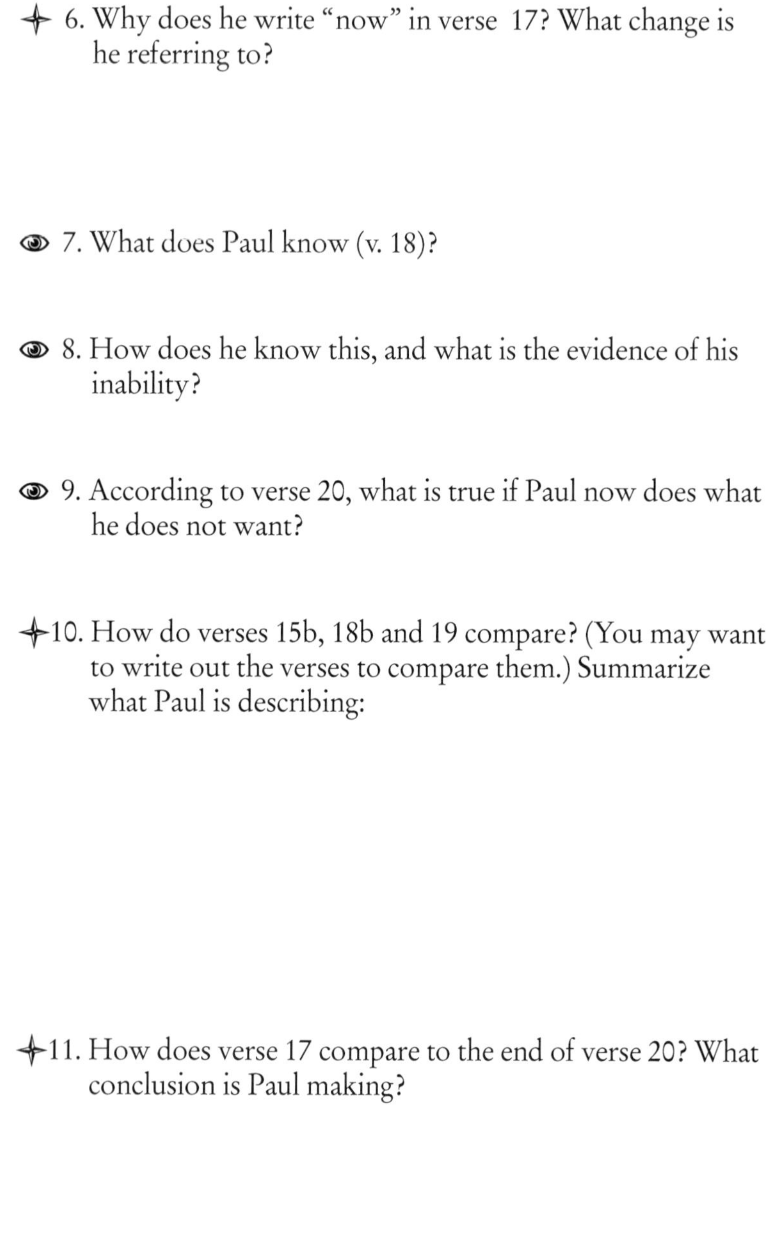

✦ 6. Why does he write "now" in verse 17? What change is he referring to?

👁 7. What does Paul know (v. 18)?

👁 8. How does he know this, and what is the evidence of his inability?

👁 9. According to verse 20, what is true if Paul now does what he does not want?

✦10. How do verses 15b, 18b and 19 compare? (You may want to write out the verses to compare them.) Summarize what Paul is describing:

✦11. How does verse 17 compare to the end of verse 20? What conclusion is Paul making?

12. If Paul is engaging in the sin, how can he say, "it is no longer I who do it, but sin that dwells within me"? Is he refusing to take responsibility for his sin? What would you point to in previous verses or chapters to explain Paul's conclusion?

13. Do you ever feel perplexed by your own actions? Are your actions (or lack of action) ever out of line with your desires? Do you ever do what you do not want to do, or neglect to do what you want to do? Explain:

14. How does it help in our battle against sin to know that as believers our sin issues are no longer *who we are* but are *forces to battle against*?

15. How does serving "in the new way of the Spirit and not in the old way of the written code" (v. 6) change the battle for us?

Pray, then read Romans 7:13–8:4.

Romans 7:21–25

👁 1. What does Paul find?

👁 2. Upon what experience does he base this?

✦ 3. What does Paul mean when he says he "delight[s] in the law of God, in [his] inner being," and how does this delight cause him to want to do right?

✦ 4. What "evil lies close at hand," and what "law [is] waging war against the law of [his] mind" making him "captive to the law of sin"?

✦ 5. How is it that this law "dwells in [his] members"? What does he mean by "members"?

👁 6. What does this situation cause him to cry out?

❤ 7. Do you feel this battle going on inside you? Are there
times when you want to cry out, "wretched woman that I
am!"? Describe your experience:

👁 8. After his exclamation, what question does Paul ask?

✦ 9. Why does he ask this question?

👁10. How does Paul answer his exasperated question?

✦11. What does Paul's thanksgiving suggest about the answer
to his question?

👁 12. How does Paul sum up chapter 7 of Romans?

✦13. What do "flesh" and "members" mean in chapter 7?
How do they relate to one another?

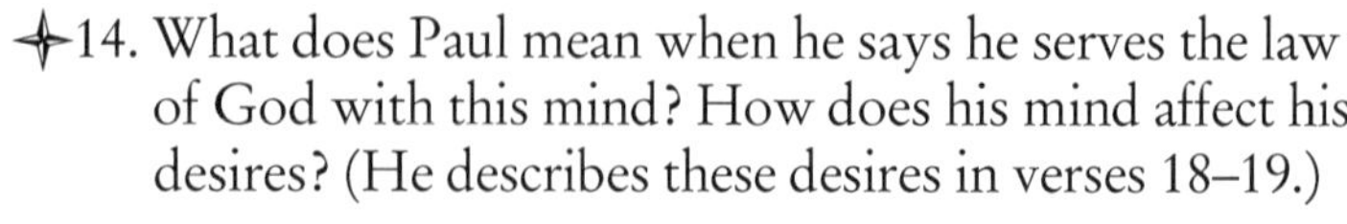

14. What does Paul mean when he says he serves the law of God with this mind? How does his mind affect his desires? (He describes these desires in verses 18–19.)

15. How would you use verses 13–25 to explain your own experience of struggling with sin in your life?

16. If you relate to Paul's argument in chapter 7, what is your only hope in life, and how would you explain that hope to a non-Christian friend?

NOTES

WEEK 16: ROMANS 8:1–13

Pray this week to gain a deeper understanding of life in Christ by the Spirit.

DAY 1

Pray, then read Romans 7:21–8:11.

Romans 8:1–2

👁 1. What is there now?

✦ 2. What is the "therefore" there for? Why does Paul here assure those who are in Christ that there is now no condemnation?

👁 3. What has the law of the Spirit of life done?

✦ 4. What does condemnation mean? Who condemns and for what? What happens as a result of condemnation? See Romans 5:12–14, 16–18.

✦ 5. What does it mean for there to be "no condemnation"?

✦ 6. Notice the words, "in Christ Jesus" in both verses 1 and 2. Who are "those who are in Christ Jesus"? See Romans 6:3–5. See also 6:6–11.

✦ 7. Why do you think Paul calls the Spirit the "Spirit of life" here, and what is "the law of the Spirit of life"? See also Romans 6:17 and 7:6.

✦ 8. What does the Spirit of life have to do with being in Christ Jesus? See also Romans 5:5.

✦ 9. What is "the law of sin and death"? See also Romans 7:8–10.

✦10. What does it mean to be set free from "the law of sin and death," and what does this have to do with "no condemnation"?

✦ 11. What is the tone of these verses?

♥12. What does it mean for your life that there is "no condemnation" in Christ Jesus and that the Spirit of life sets those in Christ Jesus free from the law of sin and death?

♥13. Can you relate to Paul's triumphant tone in this passage after the struggle of chapter 7? Explain:

DAY 2

Pray, then read Romans 8:1–11.

Romans 8:3–4

👁 1. What has God done?

👁 2. How did God do what the law could not do?

👁 3. In what likeness and for what purpose did God send his own Son?

4. What was condemned and by whom, and what was the purpose of this condemnation?

5. How do those who are in Christ fulfill the righteous requirement of the law?

6. What does verse 3b tell us about the person of Christ? See also Philippians 2:6–7.

7. How is the law "weakened by the flesh," and why could it not do what God could do? See Romans 3:20 and 7:8–11, 13.

8. In your own words, explain how God has done what the law could not do? See also John 3:16 and 2 Corinthians 5:21.

9. What is "the righteous requirement of the law"? See Matthew 22:36–40.

✦ 10. What would it mean to walk "according to the flesh"? See Romans 7:5. See also Romans 7:14, 18, 24 and Galatians 5:19–21.

✦ 11. What does it mean to walk "according to the Spirit"? See Romans 2:26, 29; 6:17; 7:6 and Galatians 5:16, 22–24. (The rest of Romans 8 will unpack this for us.)

✦ 12. In the following verses, Paul will explain the Spirit's work in the life of a Christian. According to verses 1–3, what is the basis for the Christian walking according to the Spirit?

✦ 13. How does walking according to the Spirit enable the Christian to fulfill "the righteous requirement of the law"?

♥ 14. How does the fact that God sent his own Son for you motivate you to walk according to the Spirit instead of the flesh?

15. How does the fact that God has done what the law could not do spur you on to evangelism and give you hope for family and friends who are not yet in Christ Jesus?

DAY 3

Pray, then read Romans 8:1–11.

Romans 8:5–8

1. What do "those who live according to the flesh" do?

2. What does it mean to set the mind on the things of the flesh? See also Romans 1:18, 21–23, 25 and 6:12–13.

3. But what do "those who live according to the Spirit" do?

4. What are the things of the Spirit? See Philippians 4:8 and Colossians 3:1–4.

5. What is the difference between setting the mind on the flesh and setting the mind on the Spirit?

✦ 6. Why does setting the mind on the flesh lead to death? See
Romans 6:23. See also Romans 6:16, 21 and 7:5, 13.

✦ 7. What does it mean that the mind set on the Spirit "is life
and peace"?

♥ 8. How does focusing your mind on the things of the Spirit
bring you life and peace?

◉ 9. How does the person who sets her mind on the flesh
show hostility to God?

◉10. Can the person whose mind is set on the flesh submit to
God's law?

◉11. What is Paul's conclusion about those who are in the
flesh (v. 8)?

✦12. How is God's law summed up by Jesus in Matthew
22:36–40? How does this help us explain why those

　　　　　　　　　　　　　　　Week 16

whose minds are set on the flesh cannot please God? See also James 4:4.

❤ 13. There are many people in the world who do "good" things in the flesh. They may be religious or even atheist. Why do their "good" things not please God?

❤ 14. As Christians, we almost always have mixed motives when we do good things. We want to please our heavenly Father and love our neighbors, but we also want recognition from others or some earthly reward. How can our good works, even if they are tainted by mixed motives, please God?

❤ 15. What are some things we can do to increase our desire to please God and decrease our worldly or self-centered motives? How can we increasingly set our minds on the things of the Spirit?

Pray, then read Romans 8:1–17.

Romans 8:9–11

👁 1. What makes one "not in the flesh but in the Spirit"?

👁 2. Who "does not belong to [Christ]"?

👁 3. What is true about the body, and what is true about the Spirit "if Christ is in you"?

✦ 4. In verse 9, Paul writes, "the Spirit of God dwells in you," and, in verse 10, he writes, "Christ is in you." Describe how both of these are true. See also John 14:15–18, 23.

✦ 5. What does "the body is dead because of sin" mean?

✦ 6. What does "the Spirit is life because of righteousness" if Christ is in you mean? And what righteousness is this phrase referring to?

⊙ 7. How is the Spirit described in verse 11?

✦ 8. Who is the "him" and the "he" in verse 11, and what has
he done?

⊙ 9. "If the Spirit of him who raised Jesus from the dead
dwells in you," then what will he also do?

✦10. What does it mean that "he who raised Christ Jesus from
the dead will also give life to your mortal bodies"?

✦11. How does verse 11 explain verse 10?

✦12. How do you see the three persons of the Trinity at work
in verses 10–11?

✦13. Verses 9–11 follow a discussion of why those who are in
the flesh are hostile to God and cannot please him. How

do these verses prove that those who are in the Spirit are pleasing to God?

♥ 14. If we are in Christ, our mortal bodies are dead because of sin but there is no condemnation and our bodies will ultimately be raised to new life. How does your future bodily resurrection give you life and peace now?

♥ 15. How does this give you hope even when you see sin in your life? How does it motivate you to fight that sin?

DAY 5

Pray, then read Romans 8.

Romans 8:12–13

👁 1. Paul has just written that there is "now no condemnation for those who are in Christ Jesus" but instead there is life and peace through the Spirit who indwells those who are in Christ. What does he make clear in verse 12?

✢ 2. If we are debtors but not to the flesh, to whom are we debtors and what do we owe?

3. Do you think of yourself as a debtor to God? How does remembering this affect your life?

4. What will happen if you live according to the flesh?

5. In contrast, how does one not die but live?

6. Explain who is responsible to put to death the deeds of the body and by what means?

7. What does it mean to put to death the deeds of the body, and how does one do this by the Spirit? See Romans 8:5b; Ephesians 6:17b–18a; and Hebrews 4:11–13.

8. Describe how you regularly strive to set your mind on the things of the Spirit and how this enables you to put sin to death.

♥ 9. Describe how you use the sword of the Spirit to put your sin to death. Are there times you remember fighting a specific sin with that sword?

✦10. The "ifs" in verse 13 introduce conditions to the main clauses. The main clauses are "you will die" and "you will live." In other words, the "if" clauses give us the conditions for life or death. One way leads to death and the other to life. But Paul has taught us throughout Romans that salvation is a gift from God through faith in Jesus Christ. We don't earn it through our works. How does 8:1–11 help you reconcile "The righteous shall live by faith" (Romans 1:17) with the conditional clauses in verse 13? *(Next week, we will see that what follows in Romans 8 will also help us understand what these conditional clauses mean.)*

♥11. How do verses 12–13 motivate you to fight sin in your life?

WEEK 17: ROMANS 8:14–27

Pray this week to have a deeper understanding of the glory that awaits you and for that understanding to penetrate your life in a way that gives you supernatural confidence and patience in times of suffering.

DAY 1

Pray, then read Romans 8:9–25.

Romans 8:14–15

✦ 1. How would you sum up Romans so far?

◉ 2. Why will those who "put to death the deeds of the body" live?

✦ 3. What does it mean to be led by the Spirit, and how does that correspond to putting to death the deeds of the body? See also Galatians 5:16–18.

✦ 4. Romans 8:9–11 explains that everyone who belongs to Christ has the Spirit dwelling in him or her. Verse 13 tells us that one who fights sin by the Spirit will live. Now verse 14 gives us the amazing, joyful truth that those who have the Spirit are sons of God! How does belonging to Christ correspond to being a son of God?

5. If you are a son of God, what did you not receive?

6. What would a spirit of slavery cause?

7. What have you received, and what does this cause you to cry out?

8. By whom do we Christians cry out?

9. What kind of fear would the spirit of slavery cause?

10. What is different about the Spirit of adoption, and why would Paul contrast falling "back into fear" with crying out "Abba! Father!"?

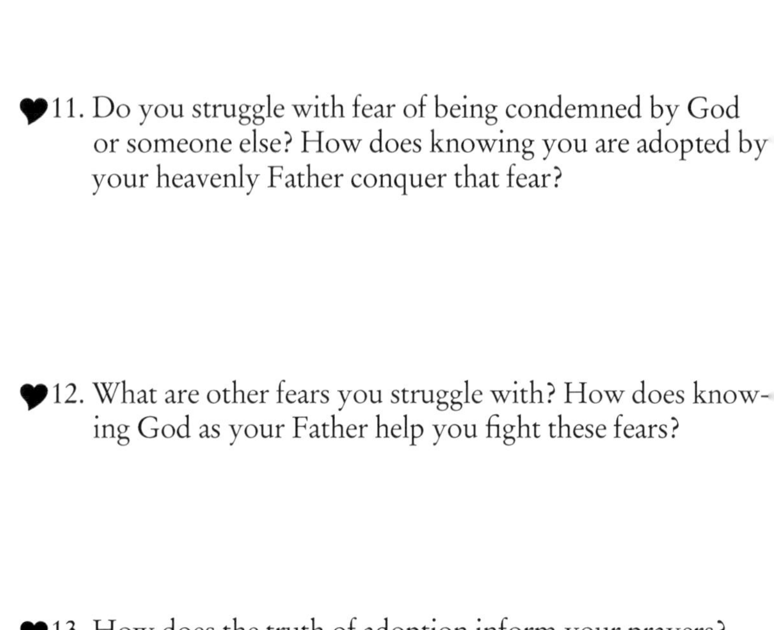

♥ 11. Do you struggle with fear of being condemned by God or someone else? How does knowing you are adopted by your heavenly Father conquer that fear?

♥ 12. What are other fears you struggle with? How does knowing God as your Father help you fight these fears?

♥ 13. How does the truth of adoption inform your prayers?

♥ 14. Do you cry out to the Father when you are in need? Do you recognize his love and goodness and willingness to help? Explain your answer.

DAY 2

Pray, then read Romans 8:12–25.

Romans 8:16–17

👁 1. What does the Spirit himself do?

✦ 2. What does it mean for the Spirit to bear "witness with
    our spirit," and what does this have to do with us crying
    "Abba! Father!"? See also Romans 5:5.

♥ 3. This is one way we know we are Christians. Do
    you experience this in your life? If so, describe your
    experience:

◉ 4. What status follows if we are children of God?

✦ 5. What does it mean to be "heirs of God," and what does it
    mean that we are "fellow heirs with Christ"? Is there an
    individual and a collective component to our inheritance?
    What do the heirs inherit? See Ephesians 1:11–14; Gala-
    tians 3:29–4:7; and Titus 3:7.

◉ 6. What is the condition for being children and heirs?

✦ 7. What does it mean to suffer with Christ?

✦ 8. How is suffering connected to being united to Christ? Explain why this condition of suffering with Christ doesn't mean that we earn our inheritance by suffering.

◉ 9. What is the purpose of suffering with Christ?

✦ 10. How is being glorified with Christ related to being an heir with him, and why would it involve suffering?

✦ 11. In what way did Christ's suffering lead to glory?

♥12. As children of God, heirs with Christ, we will inherit the new heavens and earth, where we will live with God face to face for the rest of eternity. Our inheritance is God himself! If you are a child of God, how does that inheritance affect your life now?

♥13. There is so much joy and triumph in these verses. How does the message about suffering hit you? Have you suffered with Christ? If so, what are some ways you have suffered? If not, why do you think this kind of suffering is not a part of your life?

♥14. How does the promise of being glorified with Christ in the future affect how you suffer?

DAY 3

Pray, then read Romans 8:12–27.

Romans 8:18–22

👁 1. What does Paul consider?

👁 2. What evidence does Paul give that the Christian's suffering is not even comparable to the glory that will be revealed to us?

👁 3. Why does the creation long for the revealing of the sons of God?

✦ 4. Was the creation subjected to futility willingly? Who is the one who subjected it?

👁 5. What is the hope of creation?

👁 6. What do we know about the whole creation?

✦ 7. Creation doesn't actually have emotions like "longing." It doesn't literally groan. Why does Paul personify creation in this passage? What is he trying to get across using these anthropomorphisms? What tone do they create? And what does the word "hope" tell us?

✦ 8. Who are the sons of God, and how do you know?

✦ 9. What does it mean that the sons of God will be revealed, and when will they be revealed? See 1 John 3:2. See also 1 Peter 1:3–5, 5:1.

✦10. What does it mean that creation was subjected to futility? See Genesis 3:16–19, 23–24.

♥11. What are some ways you see creation experiencing futility? How does creation groan?

✦12. Why do you think God allowed man's sin to affect all of his creation? What was man's role supposed to be? See Genesis 1:26–28.

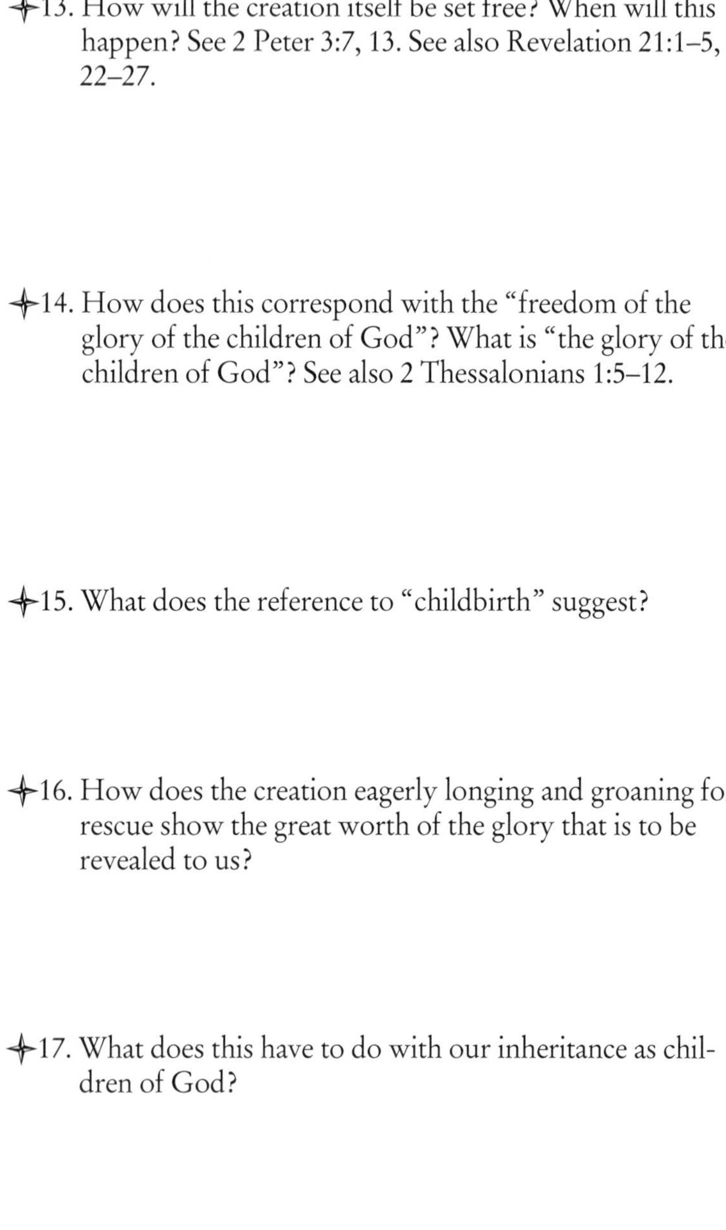

✦13. How will the creation itself be set free? When will this happen? See 2 Peter 3:7, 13. See also Revelation 21:1–5, 22–27.

✦14. How does this correspond with the "freedom of the glory of the children of God"? What is "the glory of the children of God"? See also 2 Thessalonians 1:5–12.

✦15. What does the reference to "childbirth" suggest?

✦16. How does the creation eagerly longing and groaning for rescue show the great worth of the glory that is to be revealed to us?

✦17. What does this have to do with our inheritance as children of God?

💙18. Can you express verse 18 from the heart? How does the hope of future glory affect the way you deal with suffering in the present? (Or how would you like it to affect the way you deal with suffering?)

DAY 4

Pray, then read Romans 8:16–30.

Romans 8:23–25

✦ 1. Verse 18 begins with "For." How are verses 18–25 connected to verse 17?

◉ 2. In verse 23, what do Paul and his readers do along with creation?

◉ 3. How does Paul describe himself and his readers?

✦ 4. What does it mean to "have the firstfruits of the Spirit"?

✦ 5. What does it mean to "groan inwardly"?

👁 6. What do those "who have the firstfruits of the Spirit" do while they inwardly groan?

✦ 7. What does "the redemption of our bodies" refer to?

✦ 8. Verses 14–15 say, "all who are led by the Spirit of God **are** sons of God" and "**have received** the Spirit of adoption." But verse 23 says "we **wait** eagerly for adoption as sons, the redemption of our bodies." As Christians, are we already adopted, or do we wait for adoption? Why are these verses not contradictory?

♥ 9. Do you "groan inwardly" and "wait eagerly"? What does that look like in your life?

10. According to verse 24, why do we wait eagerly?

11. In hope of what were we saved? How is hope related to salvation?

12. What is hope that is seen, and why?

13. What does hoping for what we do not see cause us to do?

14. What is Paul describing in verses 24–25? What does it mean to wait with patience?

15. As Christians, we groan inwardly and wait eagerly in hope for the redemption of our bodies. How does this relate to the previous verses about creation?

16. What does this hope for the redemption of our bodies have to do with glory?

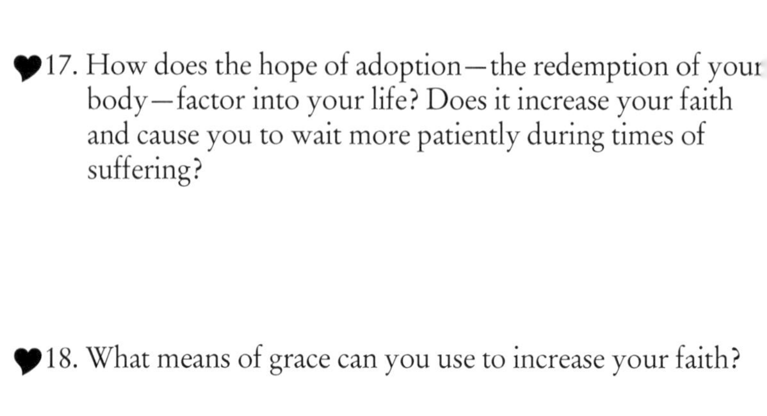

17. How does the hope of adoption—the redemption of your body—factor into your life? Does it increase your faith and cause you to wait more patiently during times of suffering?

18. What means of grace can you use to increase your faith?

DAY 5

Pray, then read Romans 8:18–30.

Romans 8:26–27

1. What does the Spirit do?

2. Why does Paul start this section with a "Likewise"?

3. What do we not know?

4. How does the Spirit help us in our weakness?

5. Why don't we know what we ought to pray for, and what does this have to do with hope-filled waiting?

✦ 6. What does it mean that the Spirit intercedes for us? With whom does he intercede?

✦ 7. What are "groanings too deep for words"? What does this phrase imply about the Spirit's care for us?

◉ 8. What does "he who searches hearts" know?

◉ 9. How does he know it?

✦10. Who is "he," and how do you know this?

✦11. What does it mean for the Spirit to intercede for the saints "according to the will of God"? What is the Spirit's goal in his prayers for us?

♥12. What does this tell us about how we should pray?

♥13. How can you grow in praying according to God's will?

♥14. Notice the creation groans (v. 22), we groan (v. 23), and the Spirit groans for us (v. 26). How does the Spirit's deep groaning give you comfort when you're struggling?

♥15. How does the Spirit's intercession according to the will of God give you confidence when you're suffering? How does it increase your hope?

♥16. How do you see the Spirit differently after studying Romans 8:1–27?

WEEK 18: ROMANS 8:28–39

Pray this week to be more firmly rooted in the love of God in Christ Jesus our Lord.

DAY 1

Pray, then read Romans 8:18–32.

Romans 8:28–29

👁 1. What do we know?

👁 2. For whom do all things work together for good?

✦ 3. There are two phrases that describe the people for whom God works everything together for good: "those who love God" and "those who are called according to his purpose." How are these two descriptions related?

👁 4. What is also true of "those whom [God] foreknew"?

👁 5. Why does God conform those whom he predestined to the image of his Son?

✦ 6. What does it mean to be "called according to [God's] purpose"? Who does the calling, and what is the purpose?

✦ 7. What does "all things work together for good" mean?
For whose good?

✦ 8. How does the phrase "work together" add to our understanding of how God works? Will we always see a silver
lining to every individual cloud in our lives, or do those
words give us a deeper understanding of the big picture of
God's work in our lives?

✦ 9. "Foreknew" means more than just prior knowledge.
What does it mean? Read Genesis 4:1; Amos 3:1–2; and 1
Peter 1:1–2, 20. See also Romans 11:1–2.

♥10. How does the word "foreknew" here give you confidence and comfort?

✦11. What does "predestined" mean? Read Ephesians 1:4–6,
11. See Romans 9:23–24. See also Acts 4:27–28.

✦12. What does it mean to be "conformed to the image of
[God's] Son," and how does this inform our understanding of how the Spirit intercedes for us according to God's
will?

✦13. God the Son is eternal and had no beginning. How then
can Paul describe him as "the firstborn among many
brothers"? To what is Paul referring? See Colossians 1:15,
18. See also Revelation 1:5.

✦14. Who are the brothers, and why must they be conformed
to the image of the Son?

✦15. What does it tell us about the greatness of Jesus Christ
   that God is conforming Christians to his likeness?

✦16. Summarize verses 28–29, and explain how they are connected to verse 18:

♥17. What is your hope when you go through suffering, and
   how does that hope affect how you pray during those
   times?

♥18. How might you use Romans 8:18–29 to help someone in
   your church go through suffering?

DAY 2

Pray, then read Romans 8:28–39.

Romans 8:30

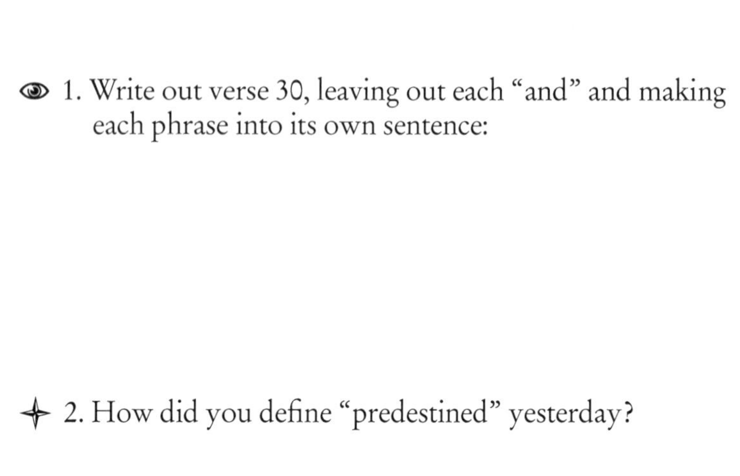

1. Write out verse 30, leaving out each "and" and making each phrase into its own sentence:

2. How did you define "predestined" yesterday?

3. What does it mean to be "called"? Who are those who are called, and how are they called? Read your answer from question 6 yesterday, and see Acts 2:39; John 10:3–5, 26–29 and Romans 1:7. See also 1 Corinthians 1:21–24; 1 Thessalonians 2:12 and 2 Thessalonians 2:14.

4. Using previous passages in Romans, explain what it means to be "justified":

✦ 5. What does it mean to be "glorified," and when does this happen? See Philippians 3:20–21 and 1 John 3:2. See also Colossians 3:4.

✦ 6. If the Christian will be glorified when she sees Christ face to face, why does Paul write "glorified" in the past tense rather than the future tense "will glorify"?

✦ 7. Who does the work of predestining, calling, justifying, and glorifying; and what do these things have to do with being "conformed to the image of [God's] Son"? See also Philippians 1:6; 1 Thessalonian 5:23–24 and 2 Peter 1:3.

♥ 8. Does anyone fall out of this loop? Are there any who are predestined by God who do not receive God's call? Or are there any whom God calls who are not justified and

ultimately glorified? If you are a Christian, how does
verse 30 affect you?

✦ 9. How does verse 30 help define the "good" in verse 28
and point us back to verse 18?

♥10. How does verse 30 boost your confidence that God is
working all things together for your good even in times
of suffering?

♥11. How does knowing your destination is glory affect your
life today?

DAY 3

Pray, then read Romans 8:28–39.

Romans 8:31–32

👁 1. What question does Paul ask?

2. What "things" is Paul referring to, and why does he ask this question?

3. With what question does Paul answer his first question?

4. How does chapter 8 show that God is "for us"?

5. Who would be against those who love God and are called according to his purpose, and what might this statement have to do with verses 17–18 and following?

6. How does verse 32 state the ultimate proof of God being for us?

7. If God "did not spare his own Son but gave him up for us all," what can we conclude?

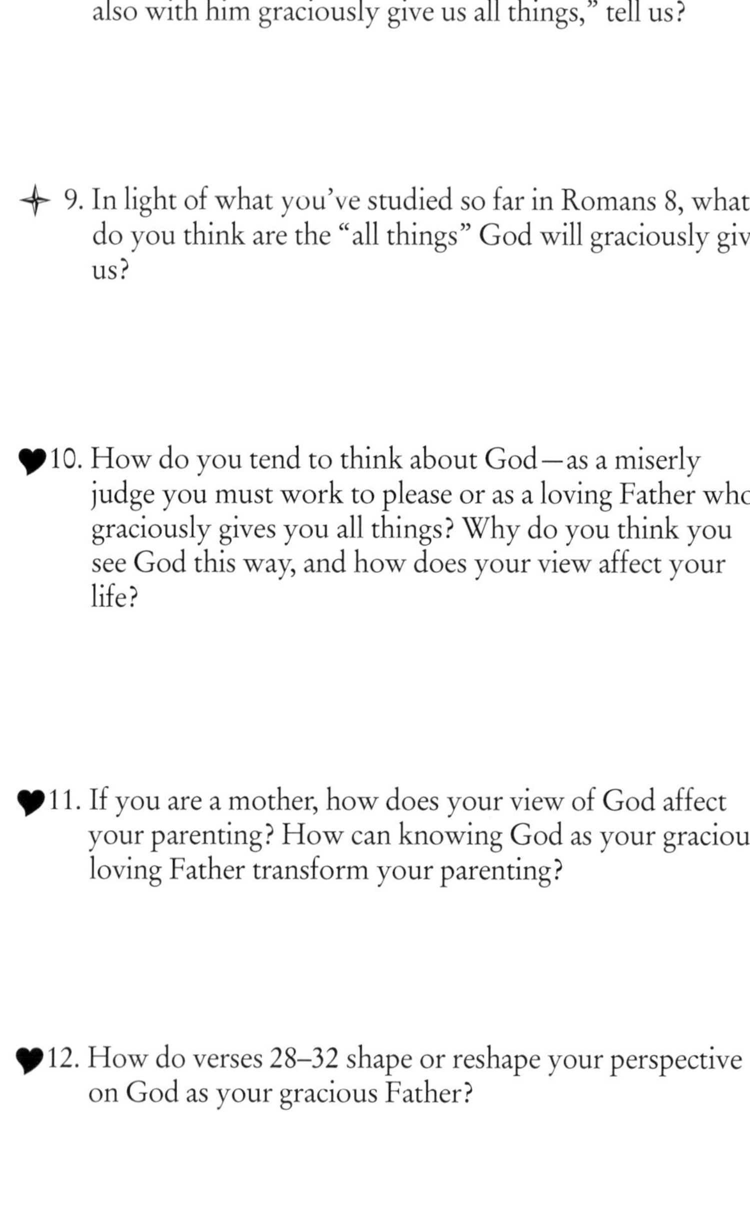

✦ 8. What does "with him" in the phrase, "how will he not also with him graciously give us all things," tell us?

✦ 9. In light of what you've studied so far in Romans 8, what do you think are the "all things" God will graciously give us?

♥10. How do you tend to think about God—as a miserly judge you must work to please or as a loving Father who graciously gives you all things? Why do you think you see God this way, and how does your view affect your life?

♥11. If you are a mother, how does your view of God affect your parenting? How can knowing God as your gracious loving Father transform your parenting?

♥12. How do verses 28–32 shape or reshape your perspective on God as your gracious Father?

Pray, then read Romans 8:31–39.

Romans 8:33–34

👁 1. What question does Paul ask?

✦ 2. How do verses 29–30 help define who God's "elect" are? See also Deuteronomy 7:6–8; Romans 9:10–12 and 1 Peter 2:9–10.

✦ 3. Who would bring a charge against God's elect? What kind of situation is Paul addressing here?

👁 4. With what statement and rhetorical question does Paul answer his previous question?

✦ 5. What point is Paul making with this statement followed by the question? What is the answer to the question, and why?

👁 6. What three truths does Paul point out about Christ Jesus in verse 34?

◉ 7. What is Jesus doing at the right hand of God?

✦ 8. What do these things have to do with justification and
     not being condemned?

✦ 9. How is this passage connected to the previous verses?

♥10. Do you ever feel condemned for something you've done
     or left undone? Has anyone ever accused you of some-
     thing and left you feeling deeply guilty? How does Christ
     Jesus's death and resurrection speak to your feelings of
     guilt and shame?

♥11. In verse 26, we saw that the Spirit, who dwells in us,
     intercedes for us. Now we see that Jesus intercedes for us
     at the right hand of God. How does this glorious truth
     help you when you are feeling condemned?

Pray, then read Romans 8:31–39.

Romans 8:35–39

👁 1. What question does Paul ask?

👁 2. In his next question, what does he list as possible circumstances that we might think would separate us from the love of Christ?

✦ 3. These are not minor inconveniences. Using a 1–5 scale with 5 being the most threatening, how would you rate the threat level for each of these circumstances?

👁 4. What Old Testament quote does Paul use to sum up the danger the Christians in Rome might face?

✦ 5. This quote is from Psalm 44:22. What is Psalm 44 about, and why would Paul quote it here? Also, for whose sake do Christians face death?

✦ 6. How does this Old Testament quote point us to Jesus? See Isaiah 53:4–7; John 1:29; and Revelation 5:5–13.

👁 7. What is Paul's answer to the question of whether even the most dire circumstances can separate us from the love of Christ? What does he say about Christians "in all these things"?

👁 8. Where does the power to conquer come from?

✦ 9. "[T]ribulation, or distress, or persecution, or famine, or nakedness, or danger, or sword"; "we are being killed all the day long." Explain what Paul means when he says, "in all these things we are more than conquerors through him who loved us."

❤ 10. Have you had the opportunity to be more than a conqueror? Describe a trial that God has used in your life.

11. What does Paul list as not being able to separate us from the love of God? For each quote below, explain *what it means* and how you would *apply* it to your life. Specifically, **what are your fears or struggles in this area and how do these verses help you in those fears and struggles?**

- "Neither death nor life" can separate us.
  - Meaning:

  - Application:

- "nor angels nor rulers"
  - Meaning:

  - Application:

- "nor things present nor things to come"
  - Meaning:

  - Application:

- "nor powers"
  - ✦ Meaning:

  ❤ Application:

- "nor height, nor depth, nor anything else in all creation"
  - ✦ Meaning:

  ❤ Application:

👁12. Through whom does the love of God come to us?

❤13. Which of the things listed in 38–39 threatens you most? How does the promise that God—who did not spare his own Son but gave him up for you—will continue to love you for eternity help you against this threat?

✦14. How is Romans 8:28–39 a fitting climax to Romans 5–8?

✦15. How is it a fitting climax to the first eight chapters of
    Romans?

ABOUT THE AUTHOR

Passionate about encouraging women to delight in the Scriptures, Keri Folmar runs women's Bible studies at the United Christian Church of Dubai where she is privileged to teach fascinating women from every inhabited continent. In addition to the *Delighting in the Word* Bible study series, she has written *The Good Portion: Scripture*, a book that encourages women to discover the treasure and enjoy the sweetness of God's word.

Keri is the wife of John, who is the senior pastor of UCCD, and they have three grown children. In a previous life, as chief counsel of House Judiciary Subcommittee on the Constitution, Keri was staff writer of the Partial Birth Abortion Ban.

cruciformpress.com

Devoted
Great Men and Their Godly Moms

Tim Challies | 128 pages

Women shaped the men who changed the world.

bit.ly/devotedbook

Majoring in Motherhood
A Crash Course in Gospel Truth for the Hardest, Messiest, Most Glorious Job in the World

Emily Schuch | 132 pages

Moms of little ones…here is the joy, humor, and rock-solid encouraging truth you need.

bit.ly/Majoring

Preparing for Marriage
Help for Christian Couples

John Piper | 86 pages

As you prepare for marriage, dare to dream with God.

bit.ly/prep-for-marriage

JERRY BRIDGES — WHO AM I? — *Our Identity in Christ*

JOHN PIPER — *Ten Essential Truths*

JONATHAN HOLMES — *Biblical Friendship*

PETER KROL — KNOWABLE WORD — *Learn to Study the Bible*

TIM CHALLIES — *Clear, Effective, Proven*

PETER KROL — SOWABLE WORD — *Learn to Lead Bible Studies*

JESSALYN HUTTO — INHERITANCE of TEARS — *God's Grace in Pregnancy Loss*

TAD THOMPSON — INTENTIONAL PARENTING — *A Simple, Functional Framework*

JOHN PIPER — *Help for Christian Couples*

ALBERT N. MARTIN — *When a Loved One Dies in Christ*

VANEETHA RENDALL RISNER — *Foreword by Joni Eareckson Tada*

PIPER, CHAN, AND 11 MORE — *30 Devotions on Marriage*